SEAFOOD

SEAFOOD

easy recipes • techniques • ingredients

MURDOCH BOOKS

contents

*Among the myriad species of fish are mighty salmon,
tuna and kingfish; magnificent reef fish such as snapper
and purple-pink pomfret; mottled creatures like ling; flounder,
sole and other curious flat fish; and the slippery eel. Take the plunge
at the fishmonger — experiment with these and other delicious
species and the many exciting ways in which to cook them.*

*The prosaic word 'shellfish' doesn't do justice to the wondrous
array of creatures that it covers. From the familiar prawns
(shrimp) and clams to luxuries such as lobster, culinary oddities
like jellyfish, and one-off wonders such as the sea urchin, there
are species enough to keep gastronomes happy for a lifetime.
Cooking with shellfish is a way to tour the world —
so head to the kitchen and enjoy your journey.*

A world of flavour

Visiting a fish market can be an exhilarating experience. So many beautifully coloured creatures of all sizes and shapes — it's wonderful to walk around just looking at each remarkable species in turn. But the very thing that makes seafood so wondrous — its great variety — also makes it harder to know where to start. The fish that sparkled so invitingly behind the fish counter can look a strange new creature indeed when lying on the kitchen bench at home.

There is little need for hesitation, however; seafood can be easy to prepare and cook, and cooking with it is one of the best ways to explore other cultures and cuisines. As to the tricky gutting and scaling of fish, well, that is what fishmongers are for. The main requirement of fish and shellfish is freshness. For best possible results, buy seafood on the day of eating or, at the most, the day before. But this is not an insurmountable problem — most large supermarkets have fresh seafood counters and local fishmongers and markets are springing up — give them a try, ask questions, build up a relationship with the staff. You'll soon know who is the best informed and most passionate about their product.

Seafood makes up the world's most numerous and diverse group of 'wild' food stocks, and can be found in all the waters of the world — but it is a delicate, finite resource. Unfortunately, in recent decades there has been increasing pressure on worldwide fish stocks through overfishing, damage to marine habitats and wasteful fishing practices such as bycatch. This refers to the unwanted fish (including young fish), marine mammals, turtles and seabirds caught during fishing for commercial stocks. If this concerns you, numerous local and international groups will happily provide information about which fish species are and are not endangered. There are also many positive developments, such as the establishment of the Marine Stewardship Council, a non-profit, international organization that allows sustainable fisheries to label their products with their logo. Farmed stocks are another option. Fisheries now produce delicious and environmentally friendly farmed kingfish, rainbow trout, mussels and clams.

The recipes in this book have been chosen to demonstrate how easily seafood can become an exciting and nutritious part of everyday cooking and to show how seafood is at the heart of so many cuisines around the world. So don't be intimidated by the dazzling variety at the fish market — wade in, ask questions, take your prize home, then experiment in the kitchen and enjoy the rewards.

fish

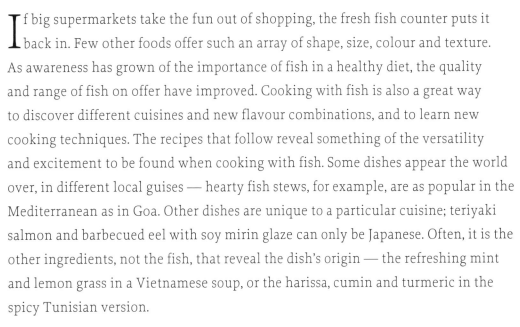

If big supermarkets take the fun out of shopping, the fresh fish counter puts it back in. Few other foods offer such an array of shape, size, colour and texture. As awareness has grown of the importance of fish in a healthy diet, the quality and range of fish on offer have improved. Cooking with fish is also a great way to discover different cuisines and new flavour combinations, and to learn new cooking techniques. The recipes that follow reveal something of the versatility and excitement to be found when cooking with fish. Some dishes appear the world over, in different local guises — hearty fish stews, for example, are as popular in the Mediterranean as in Goa. Other dishes are unique to a particular cuisine; teriyaki salmon and barbecued eel with soy mirin glaze can only be Japanese. Often, it is the other ingredients, not the fish, that reveal the dish's origin — the refreshing mint and lemon grass in a Vietnamese soup, or the harissa, cumin and turmeric in the spicy Tunisian version.

When buying fish, it can be tempting to choose safe-looking fillets and cutlets, but it is far easier to determine whether a fish is fresh by looking at a whole specimen. You can check that the fish smells of the sea — it should not smell 'fishy' — that the flesh is firm, the scales are shiny, and the eyes are clear and bright. Really fresh fish may have gaping mouths and open gill flaps, and some fish, such as salmon and trout, are covered in a clear slime (old slime is opaque). When you do want to buy fillets, if possible buy from a whole fish, asking your fishmonger to scale, gut, fillet and, if necessary, skin it for you.

A common misconception about cooking with fish is that it is high risk. Fish do cook quickly, so they need to be watched, but this short cooking time should be seen as an advantage. Many fish are excellent marinated, making them perfect for entertaining, as much work can be done in advance, or they can be cooked on the barbecue with little or no preparation. The key is to choose the right fish for the cooking technique and to do as much preparation as possible before cooking, so that you don't get distracted at the crucial moment. Firm fish such as salmon and oily fish such as tuna, sardines and mackerel are great for the barbecue; sole and whiting are classic choices for the pan; and blue eye cod, john dory, sea bass, snapper and bream are all very adaptable and can be fried, steamed or baked. Or, if you're seeking a challenge, try making sushi hand-rolls or home-made seafood lasagne; your efforts will be well rewarded.

Most recipes in this chapter give suggestions for substitute fish if the exact fish is not available. Always choose good-quality fish, then let the fish do the rest.

Smoked tuna and white bean salad

SERVES 4

Canned tuna is possibly the ultimate convenience seafood, always at the ready for sandwiches, salads or quick pasta sauces. Smoked fillets are particularly delicious. This Mediterranean-inspired salad is simple yet substantial, perfect for a summer lunch.

rocket (arugula)	100 g (3½ oz/1 small bunch)
red capsicum (pepper)	1 small, cut into thin batons
red onion	1 small, finely sliced
canned cannellini beans	310 g (11 oz), drained and rinsed
cherry tomatoes	125 g (4½ oz), cut into halves
capers	2 tablespoons, rinsed and squeezed dry
canned smoked tuna slices in oil	250 g (9 oz), drained
bread	to serve

basil dressing

lemon juice	1 tablespoon
white wine vinegar	1 tablespoon
extra virgin olive oil	60 ml (2 fl oz/¼ cup)
garlic	1 clove, crushed
basil	2 tablespoons chopped
sugar	½ teaspoon

Trim any long stems from the rocket, rinse, pat dry and divide among 4 serving plates.

Lightly toss the capsicum in a large bowl with the onion, beans, tomatoes and capers. Spoon some of this mixture onto the rocket on each plate, then scatter some tuna over each.

To make the dressing, thoroughly whisk all the ingredients in a bowl with 1 tablespoon water, ¼ teaspoon salt and freshly ground black pepper to taste. Drizzle over the salad and serve immediately with bread.

Fish substitution fresh tuna, seared on both sides and sliced, or tinned salmon

Remove the membranes and seeds from the capsicum.

Slice the capsicum into thin batons.

Whisk together all the ingredients for the basil dressing.

Thai fish cakes

SERVES 4–6

These classic Thai appetizers are quick and easy to make in a food processor. They typically have a puffy appearance and are firm and slightly chewy. Their flavour is mildly spicy; if you prefer a bit more heat, increase the quantity of red curry paste according to your taste.

firm white fish fillets, such as ling, cod or hake	450 g (1 lb) skinned
rice flour	45 g (1½ oz/¼ cup)
fish sauce	1 tablespoon
egg	1, lightly beaten
coriander (cilantro) leaves	3 tablespoons
red curry paste	3 teaspoons
red chillies	1–2 teaspoons, chopped (optional)
green beans	100 g (3½ oz), very thinly sliced
spring onions (scallions)	2, finely chopped
oil	for frying
sweet chilli sauce	to serve
chopped peanuts and finely diced cucumber	to garnish (optional)

Roughly chop the fish into chunks, then process in a food processor for 20 seconds, or until smooth.

Add rice flour, fish sauce, egg, coriander leaves, curry paste and the chillies, if using. Process for 10 seconds, or until well combined, then transfer to a large bowl. Alternatively, finely chop and blend by hand. Mix in the green beans and spring onion. With wet hands, form 2 tablespoons of mixture at a time into flattish patties about 5 cm (2 inches) in diameter.

Heat the oil in a heavy-based frying pan over medium heat. Cook four fish cakes at a time until golden brown on both sides. Drain on crumpled paper towels, then serve with sweet chilli sauce. The sauce can be garnished with a sprinkle of chopped peanuts and finely diced cucumber, if you wish.

Roughly chop the fish fillets into large chunks.

Put the fish into a food processor and process until smooth.

Using wet hands, form the mixture into flattish patties.

Sardines with Caesar salad

SERVES 4

Here, the anchovies usually included in Caesar salad are combined with crumbed, fried sardines. Scaled and butterflied sardines are available in vacuum packs at some fishmongers. Instructions are given below for preparing your own, or ask your fishmonger to do it for you.

dressing

egg	1
garlic	2 cloves
lemon juice	2 tablespoons
worcestershire sauce	½ teaspoon
anchovy fillets	3–4
extra virgin olive oil	125 ml (4 fl oz/½ cup)
dry breadcrumbs	100 g (3½ oz/1 cup)
parmesan cheese	65 g (2¼ oz/⅔ cup) grated
flat-leaf (Italian) parsley	2 tablespoons chopped
eggs	2, lightly beaten
milk	80 ml (2½ fl oz/⅓ cup)
sardines	16, scaled and butterflied
oil	for deep-frying
poppadoms	12 small
baby cos (romaine) lettuce	2, leaves separated
prosciutto	8 slices, cooked until crisp, then broken into pieces
parmesan cheese	50 g (1¾ oz/½ cup) shaved

To make the dressing, put the egg in a food processor, add the garlic, lemon juice, worcestershire sauce and anchovies and process to combine. With the motor running, add oil in a thin, steady stream until dressing has thickened slightly. Set aside.

Put breadcrumbs, grated parmesan and parsley in a bowl and mix well. Put beaten eggs and milk in another bowl and whisk well. Dip sardines into the egg wash, then into crumb mixture, and put on a paper-lined baking tray. Refrigerate for 1 hour.

Heat oil in a deep-fryer or heavy-based frying pan to 180°C (350°F), or until a cube of white bread dropped into the oil browns in 15 seconds. Deep-fry poppadoms until crisp, drain on paper towels, then break into pieces. Deep-fry sardines in batches until crisp and golden.

Arrange lettuce, prosciutto, poppadoms and shaved parmesan on serving plates, drizzle with dressing, then top with sardines.

Fish substitution small herring, mackerel

Sleek, silver sardines belong to the herring family, which also includes anchovies. Sardines are found all over the world, but are particularly popular in the Mediterranean. They are fairly fatty, so are ideal for barbecuing. They can also be marinated, baked, stuffed, smoked or canned. Sardines can be butterflied by boning through the back or the belly, with the head left on or removed. To butterfly sardines through the back, lay the scaled fish on its side and cut from head to the tail along its back with a sharp knife, keeping the knife flat against the bones. Repeat on the other side, taking care not to cut through the belly. Snip the bones at the tail and head, pull the bones free and remove guts. Pat clean.

Marinated herrings

Marinated herrings are a popular snack in the Netherlands, Belgium and Scandinavia. They are often eaten raw, after marination in an acidic mixture that serves to 'cold-cook' them. In this recipe, however, they are baked. They make a delicious light lunch with brown bread and butter.

herrings	4, filleted
pickling spice	1 tablespoon
bay leaves	2
black peppercorns	6
onion	1, cut in half lengthways and thinly sliced
white wine vinegar	200 ml (7 fl oz)
brown sugar	1 teaspoon
grain mustard	1 tablespoon
tarragon	2 tablespoons chopped
brown bread and butter	to serve

Preheat the oven to 150°C (300°F/Gas 2). Season the herring fillets with salt and pepper. Roll each fillet up, secure with a toothpick and place in a single layer in a baking dish that is just large enough to hold the rolled herrings.

Put the pickling spice, bay leaves, peppercorns, onion, vinegar and sugar into a saucepan with 400 ml (14 fl oz) water and bring to the boil. Remove the pan from the heat and stir in the mustard and tarragon.

Pour the liquid over the rolled herring fillets. Cover with foil and bake in the preheated oven for 45 minutes. Allow to cool completely in the liquid before removing them from the marinade and serving cold with brown bread and butter.

Fish substitution mackerel fillets

Roll up the fillets and secure each with a toothpick.

Stir the mustard and tarragon into the pickling liquid.

three ways with salmon

Versatile and delicious, salmon can be served raw, cooked or smoked. Smoked salmon is now readily available in supermarkets. It's not cheap, but a little goes a long way and transforms a simple salad, such as this rocket dish, into something special. If serving salmon raw, as for the carpaccio below, buy the freshest, best quality salmon you can find. Salmon with a rich, sticky teriyaki marinade makes for a quick, elegant dinner with a Japanese touch.

SMOKED SALMON AND ROCKET SALAD

To make the dressing, thoroughly whisk together 2 tablespoons extra virgin olive oil and 1 tablespoon balsamic vinegar in a bowl. Season to taste. Trim the long stems from 150 g (5½ oz/1 bunch) rocket (arugula). Rinse the leaves, pat dry and gently toss in a bowl with the dressing. Cut 1 avocado into 12 wedges. Put 3 wedges on each serving plate. Divide 250 g (9 oz) smoked salmon slices and the rocket among the plates. Scatter 325 g (11½ oz) drained and crumbled marinated goat's cheese and 2 tablespoons roughly chopped roasted hazelnuts over the top. Season with freshly ground black pepper. Serves 4.

Fish substitution smoked trout

SALMON CARPACCIO

Wrap a 500 g (1 lb 2 oz) sashimi-grade piece of salmon in foil and freeze for 20–30 minutes, or until partly frozen. Meanwhile, score a cross in the base of 3 vine-ripened tomatoes. Cover with boiling water for 30 seconds, then plunge into cold water. Drain and peel. Cut each tomato in half, scoop out the seeds with a teaspoon and dice the flesh. Put the flesh in a bowl and stir in 1 tablespoon chopped dill and 1 tablespoon baby capers, rinsed and squeezed dry. Remove the salmon from the freezer and unwrap. Using a very sharp knife or a mandolin, carefully slice the salmon thinly across the grain. Cover four serving plates with a thin layer of the slices. Whisk together 1 tablespoon extra virgin olive oil, 1 tablespoon lime juice and a large pinch of sea salt. Drizzle over the salmon just before serving. Season with freshly ground pepper and serve immediately with the tomato mixture and crusty bread. Serves 4.

Fish substitution fresh tuna, smoked salmon

TERIYAKI SALMON

In a pitcher, mix together 80 ml (2½ fl oz/⅓ cup) soy sauce, 80 ml (2½ fl oz/⅓ cup) sake, 80 ml (2½ fl oz/⅓ cup) mirin, 1 teaspoon sesame oil, 2 tablespoons brown sugar, 2 teaspoons finely grated fresh ginger and 1 crushed small garlic clove. Put 4 x 200 g (7 oz) salmon fillets in a shallow non-metallic dish and pour the marinade over them. Turn the fillets in the marinade so that they are well coated. Cover and leave to marinate in the refrigerator for at least 3 hours. Heat 1 tablespoon oil in a large heavy-based frying pan. Remove the salmon from the marinade and drain on paper towels. Fry the salmon in the oil until browned on each side, then reduce the heat and cook for 3 minutes more, or until the salmon is just cooked through. Add the marinade and bring to a simmer, remove the fish and simmer the sauce until it is thick and sticky. Return the salmon to the pan, quickly coat with the sauce and then transfer to serving plates. Garnish with 2 trimmed and chopped spring onions (scallions) and serve with rice. Serves 4.

Fish substitution ocean trout

smoked salmon and rocket salad

Barbecued eel with soy mirin glaze

SERVES 4

Freshwater eel cooked under the grill (broiler) or on the barbecue and coated with a sweet soy sauce glaze is tender and delicious. If the fillets are long and you are using the barbecue, put a skewer sideways through both ends of each fillet; this will make them easier to turn.

Japanese soy sauce	80 ml (2½ fl oz/⅓ cup)
mirin	80 ml (2½ fl oz/⅓ cup)
caster (superfine) sugar	2 tablespoons
cucumber	¼
daikon	¼
freshwater eel fillets	4 x 150–175 g (5½–6 oz), skinned
cooked white rice	to serve

Put the soy sauce, mirin and caster sugar into a small saucepan. Bring the liquid slowly to the boil and heat for 5–6 minutes until the liquid has reduced by approximately half and is thick and syrupy. Remove the pan from the heat. Preheat the grill (broiler) or barbecue flatplate to high.

Meanwhile, peel and finely shred the cucumber and daikon. Mix together.

Cook the eel for 2 minutes on each side, then brush liberally with the sauce. Continue to cook for a further 2–3 minutes on each side. Turn the eel frequently, brushing with the sauce to create a glaze. Serve the eel with the shredded cucumber and daikon garnish.

Fish substitution mackerel

With a large, sharp knife, remove roots and stem from the daikon.

Peel and finely shred the cucumber and daikon.

Brush the eel liberally with the glaze while cooking.

Fish kebabs with lemon and herb yoghurt   SERVES 4

Use any firm, meaty fish fillets, such as tuna, flake, swordfish, kingfish or barramundi, for this quick and easy recipe with Mediterranean flavours. If you are using bamboo skewers, soak them in cold water beforehand to ensure that they will not burn.

firm fish fillets	800 g (1 lb 12 oz) skinned, cut into 3 cm (1¼ inch) chunks
lemon juice	80 ml (2½ fl oz/⅓ cup)
olive oil	80 ml (2½ fl oz/⅓ cup)
bay leaves	3
cherry tomatoes	16 whole, or 2 firm tomatoes, cut into 8 wedges
red onions	2 small, cut into 8 wedges
red or orange capsicums (peppers)	2 small, seeded and cut into 8 chunks

lemon and herb yoghurt

Greek-style yoghurt	200 g (7 oz/heaped ¾ cup)
lemon juice	3 teaspoons
paprika	a pinch
mint	1 tablespoon finely chopped
flat-leaf (Italian) parsley	1 tablespoon finely chopped

couscous

instant couscous	400 g (14 oz)
fish or vegetable stock	400 ml (14 fl oz), brought to the boil
olive oil	1 tablespoon
butter	30 g (1 oz)

Put the fish chunks in a non-metallic bowl with the lemon juice, olive oil and bay leaves. Toss to mix, cover and leave to marinate for about 30 minutes in the refrigerator.

To make the lemon and herb yoghurt, put all the ingredients in a small bowl and whisk together. Refrigerate until needed.

On each of 8 metal skewers, or bamboo skewers that have been soaked for 30 minutes, thread 3 or 4 chunks of fish, 1 cherry tomato, 2 pieces of onion and 2 pieces of capsicum, alternating between the fish and the various vegetables as you go.

Preheat a barbecue flatplate or chargrill pan to high. Brush the kebabs lightly with oil, then cook for 8–10 minutes. Baste with the remaining marinade as they cook, and turn every now and then. When ready, the fish should be firm and opaque and the vegetables slightly charred.

Meanwhile, put couscous into a heatproof bowl, add stock the and oil, cover tightly and leave to sit for 5 minutes or according to the manufacturer's directions. Fluff grains with a fork and then stir in the butter. Serve kebabs on a mound of couscous, accompanied by the yoghurt dressing.

Seed the capsicum and then chop it into chunks.

Toss together the fish, lemon juice, olive oil and bay leaves.

Thread alternating chunks of fish and vegetables onto skewers.

Sugar-cured salmon

The salmon fillets are cured using a sugar, salt and herb mixture over a period of two days. This recipe is similar to the traditional Scandinavian dish of gravlax. Like gravlax, it is eaten raw and served with a mustard sauce.

middle salmon fillet	1 x 450 g (1 lb) piece, skinned
brown sugar	250 g (9 oz)
coarse sea salt	250 g (9 oz)
black peppercorns	8, lightly crushed
dill	1 tablespoon chopped
tarragon	1 tablespoon chopped
basil	1 tablespoon shredded

mustard sauce

egg yolks	3, at room temperature
light olive oil	150 ml (5 fl oz)
peanut oil	150 ml (5 fl oz)
zest	of 1 lemon, finely grated
lemon juice	1 tablespoon
dill	3 tablespoons chopped
wholegrain mustard	2 teaspoons
thick (double/heavy) cream	80 ml (2½ fl oz/⅓ cup)

cucumber salad

Lebanese (short) cucumber	1, finely sliced
dill	1 tablespoon finely chopped
extra virgin olive oil	2 teaspoons
white wine vinegar	1 teaspoon

Place the salmon on a board and check for bones. If there are any bones left in the salmon it will be impossible to slice the fish thinly as they will catch on the knife. Any small stubborn bones can be removed using tweezers.

Mix sugar and salt together and spoon half of the mixture into a shallow rectangular non-metallic dish large enough to hold the salmon. Place fish on the mixture. Sprinkle dill, peppercorns, tarragon and basil over the fish. Cover with the remaining sugar and salt mixture. Cover loosely with plastic wrap and place a tray, small board or plate on top of the fish weighed down with a couple of tins. Refrigerate for 2 days, turning the fish over in the mixture every 12 hours.

To make the sauce, place egg yolks in a medium-sized bowl with a generous pinch of salt and freshly ground black pepper, and gently whisk together. Mix the oils together in a pitcher. Slowly add oil to the egg yolks, drop by drop, whisking all the time. Increase to a slow trickle as the sauce thickens.

Fold in the lemon zest and juice, dill and mustard. Whisk the cream to the floppy stage and fold that in too. Taste and season with extra salt and pepper if desired.

To make the cucumber salad, combine the cucumber, dill, olive oil and lemon juice in a bowl and toss lightly to coat.

Remove fish from the dish and brush off the sugar and salt. Discard any brine. Using a sharp knife and cutting along the length of the piece of salmon, slice into paper-thin pieces and serve with the mustard sauce and cucumber salad. The sugar-cured salmon will keep in the refrigerator for 2 days.

Fish substitution ocean trout

three ways with fish soup

Harissa, a fiery mixture of up to 20 spices, is used in Middle Eastern and North African cooking. Here it flavours a spicy soup from Tunisia. Sour-tasting sauces and soups such as this recipe are common to Vietnamese cooking, as is the addition of herbs, particularly mint and lemon grass. The vermicelli fish soup is a popular dish from Laos; it is served in the middle or at the end of a meal, or even at breakfast time. This recipe works well with any firm white fish.

TUNISIAN FISH SOUP

Heat 60 ml (2 fl oz/$\frac{1}{4}$ cup) olive oil in a large saucepan, add 1 chopped onion and 1 chopped celery stalk and cook for 8–10 minutes, or until softened. Add 4 crushed garlic cloves and cook for a further minute. Stir in 2 tablespoons tomato paste (concentrated purée), $1\frac{1}{2}$ teaspoons ground turmeric, $1\frac{1}{2}$ teaspoons ground cumin and 2 teaspoons harissa and cook, stirring constantly, for 30 seconds. Pour 1 litre (35 fl oz/4 cups) fish stock into the saucepan and add 2 bay leaves. Bring to the boil, reduce the heat to low and simmer gently for 15 minutes. Add 200 g (7 oz/1 cup) orzo or other small pasta to the liquid and cook for about 10 minutes, or until al dente. Cut 500 g (1 lb 2 oz) mixed skinned snapper and sea bass fillets into bite-sized chunks and add to liquid. Poach gently for 3–4 minutes, or until fish is opaque. Stir in 2 tablespoons chopped mint and 2 tablespoons lemon juice, season to taste with salt, then serve with warm pitta bread. Garnish with a few extra mint leaves, if desired. Serves 6.

VIETNAMESE SOUR FISH SOUP

Cut 450 g (1 lb) filleted and skinned fish such as snapper, cod or trigger fish into bite-sized pieces. Cover and then refrigerate until required. Meanwhile, score a cross in the base of 2 vine-ripened tomatoes. Cover with boiling water for 30 seconds, then plunge into cold water. Drain and peel the skin away from the cross. Cut each tomato into 8 pieces. Heat 60 ml (2 fl oz/$\frac{1}{4}$ cup) oil in a large saucepan and when hot, add 1 finely chopped large garlic clove, 2 finely sliced shallots, 1 finely chopped stem lemon grass (white part only) and 200 g (7 oz) carrot, peeled and cut into thin batons 6 cm ($2\frac{1}{2}$ inches) long. Cook on medium heat for 10 minutes or until softened, stirring occasionally. Add 750 ml (26 fl oz/3 cups) fish stock or water, 2 tablespoons tamarind purée, 1 teaspoon of sambal oelek or other chilli sauce, 60 ml (2 fl oz/$\frac{1}{4}$ cup) fish sauce and $\frac{1}{4}$ teaspoon sugar. Bring to the boil and then reduce the heat to low and simmer for 5 minutes. Add fish and tomato pieces, 100 g ($3\frac{1}{2}$ oz) bean sprouts and 2 trimmed and finely shredded spring onions (scallions). Cook for a further 5 minutes, or until the fish is opaque. Stir in the juice of 1 lime, 2 tablespoons roughly chopped roasted peanuts and 3 tablespoons chopped Vietnamese mint. Serves 4.

VERMICELLI FISH SOUP

Cut 400 g (14 oz) firm white fish fillets such as cod, sea bass, haddock, halibut, perch or bream into thick strips. Cover and refrigerate until needed. Put 50 g ($1\frac{3}{4}$ oz) bean thread or rice vermicelli in a bowl and cover with boiling water. Leave to soak for 10 minutes, or until completely tender, then drain and cut into short lengths. Meanwhile, put 400 ml (14 fl oz) fish stock in a large saucepan and bring to the boil. Reduce the heat to low and add 300 ml ($10\frac{1}{2}$ fl oz) coconut milk and simmer for 5 minutes. Add 100 g ($3\frac{1}{2}$ oz) thinly sliced mushrooms and 1 thinly sliced small red chilli. Cook for 30 seconds, then add the fish and 50 g ($1\frac{3}{4}$ oz) shredded young spinach leaves. Poach for 2 minutes. Carefully stir in the noodles, along with 1 tablespoon soy sauce, 2 tablespoons fish sauce, the zest and juice of 1 lime, 50 g ($1\frac{3}{4}$ oz) bean sprouts, 50 g ($1\frac{3}{4}$ oz) thinly sliced cucumber, 2 trimmed and chopped spring onions (scallions) and 2 tablespoons chopped mint. Heat through and serve. Serves 6.

tunisian fish soup

Sushi hand-rolls

SERVES 4

Nori (or laver) is an edible seaweed that is greatly appreciated by the Japanese. Nori is sold dried in paper-thin sheets or in flakes. It is used for wrapping sushi, shredded into soups or crumbled onto rice. The sheets should be gently toasted before use to release the delicate sweet flavour.

sushi rice	200 g (7 oz)
rice vinegar	2 tablespoons
caster sugar	a generous pinch
very fresh fish, such as salmon fillet or tuna	175 g (6 oz), skinned
nori (dried seaweed)	6 sheets, each 20 x 18 cm (8 x 7 inches), toasted
avocado	1 small
lemon juice	1 tablespoon
wasabi paste	to taste
pickled daikon	60 g (2¼ oz)
cucumber	80 g (2¾ oz), cut into thin strips
Japanese soy sauce	to serve
pickled ginger	to serve

Rinse rice under cold running water until it runs clear. Put the rice into a saucepan with 200 ml (7 fl oz) cold water. Cover pan, bring to the boil, reduce the heat and simmer for 10 minutes.

Meanwhile, combine ¼ teaspoon of salt and 1 tablespoon of vinegar and sugar. When rice is cooked, remove from the heat and let it stand, covered, for 10 minutes. Transfer to a mixing bowl. Gradually add rice vinegar mixture, turning and folding rice using a wooden spoon or spatula, until rice is cool. Cover with a damp tea towel and then set aside; do not refrigerate.

Cut the fish into 16 pieces, about 2 cm x 5 cm x 3 mm (¾ x 2 x ⅛ inches). Cut each sheet of nori in half. Thinly slice the avocado and sprinkle with lemon juice. Mix the remaining tablespoon of vinegar with 3 tablespoons of water in a small bowl. Use this mixture to stop the rice sticking to your fingers as you form the sushi. Mould 1 tablespoon of rice at a time into oval shapes—you should end up with 16.

Holding a piece of nori in the palm of your hand, smear a little wasabi over it, place an oval of rice on top and top with a piece each of fish, avocado, daikon and cucumber. Wrap the seaweed around the filling in a cone shape, using a couple of grains of cooked rice as glue to secure the rolls. Alternatively, place the ingredients on the table for guests to help themselves. Serve the sushi with soy sauce, extra wasabi and pickled ginger.

Mould 1 tablespoon of rice at a time into an oval shape.

Top the rice with the fish, avocado, daikon and cucumber.

Roll the nori around the filling to form a neat cone.

Barbecued salmon cutlets

SERVES 4

This recipe is the work of minutes — perfect for a quick yet impressive meal. Be careful not to overcook the fish, or it will be dry; it should still be a little pink in the centre. Ask your fishmonger for a cut from the centre of the fillet, as this is the best part.

Lebanese (short) cucumbers	2 small, peeled, seeded and finely diced
red onion	1, finely chopped
red chilli	1, finely chopped
pickled ginger	2 tablespoons, shredded
rice vinegar	2 tablespoons
sesame oil	½ teaspoon
salmon cutlets	4
nori (dried seaweed)	1 sheet, toasted, thinly sliced
steamed rice	to serve

To make the cucumber dressing, combine the cucumber, onion, chilli, ginger, rice vinegar and sesame oil in a bowl, cover and set aside at room temperature while you cook the salmon cutlets.

Preheat a barbecue flatplate or chargrill pan to high. Lightly brush the salmon cutlets with oil. Cook the salmon on the barbecue or pan for about 2 minutes on each side, or until cooked as desired. Serve the salmon topped with the cucumber dressing and sprinkled with the strips of toasted nori. Serve with steamed rice.

Fish substitution ocean trout cutlets

Peel, seed and finely dice the cucumbers.

Using scissors, cut the toasted nori sheet into thin strips.

Cook the fish until just done and still slightly pink in the centre.

Salmon on skordalia with saffron

There are many versions of skordalia, a greek dish based on bread or potatoes, olive oil and garlic. Here it forms a bed for salmon with a zesty butter sauce. Mash the potatoes with a potato masher; using a food processor will produce a gluey consistency.

skordalia

potatoes	500 g (1 lb 2 oz), peeled and diced
garlic	3 cloves, finely chopped
lime juice	2 tablespoons
milk	100 ml (3½ fl oz)
extra virgin olive oil	150 ml (5 fl oz)

saffron and lime butter

butter	100 g (3½ oz)
saffron threads	a pinch
lime juice	2 tablespoons
salmon fillets	4 x 200 g (7 oz)
oil	2 tablespoons
lime zest	1 tablespoon grated, to garnish
chervil leaves	to garnish

To make the skordalia, bring a large saucepan of water to the boil, add the potato and cook for 10 minutes, or until very soft. Drain thoroughly and mash until quite smooth. Stir the garlic, lime juice and milk into the potato, then gradually pour in the oil, mixing well with a wooden spoon.

To make saffron and lime butter, melt the butter in a small saucepan, add the saffron and lime juice and cook until the butter turns a nutty brown colour. Remove from the heat.

Pat the salmon fillets dry. Heat the oil in a frying pan and cook the salmon, skin side down, over high heat for 2–3 minutes, or until skin is crisp and golden. Turn over and cook for a further 2–3 minutes. Serve the salmon on a bed of the skordalia, with the saffron and lime butter drizzled over the top. Garnish with lime zest and chervil leaves.

Fish substitution ocean trout

The most expensive spice in the world, saffron is the orange-red stigma hand-picked from the flower of one species of crocus, then dried. It has a pungent and aromatic flavour and an intense colour. It is added to butters and sauces such as hollandaise and aïoli, and is a lovely complement to shellfish. Bouillabaisse, paella, the pilaffs of India and Persian dishes all feature saffron. The best comes from Spain, Iran and Kashmir. Both thread and powder forms are available, but threads are preferable, as the powder can be adulterated with cheaper spices. To use, soak threads in warm water for a few minutes to infuse, then strain the liquid or add both the liquid and the threads to the dish.

Fish terrine

SERVES 4

This terrine has a soft texture and is lightly flavoured with dill and chives. It makes an elegant first course. Serve each slice sprinkled with a little caviar and accompanied by a clean-tasting salad, such as watercress and cucumber, rather than bread or toasts.

pike fillet	400 g (14 oz), skinned
egg whites	2 large
thick (double/heavy) cream	225 ml (8 fl oz)
lemon juice	1 tablespoon
dill	1 tablespoon chopped
chives	1 teaspoon chopped
ground nutmeg	a pinch
salmon fillet	110 g (3¾ oz), skinned
salmon roe	to garnish (optional)
Lebanese (short) cucumber	1, thinly sliced lengthways, to garnish (optional)
watercress	a handful, to garnish (optional)
dill sprigs	to garnish (optional)

Cut the pike into bite-sized pieces and chill well.

Prepare a loaf tin 22 x 7 x 7 cm (8½ x 2¾ x 2¾ inches) by lining it with baking paper and then lightly oiling the paper. Using a food processor, blend the pike to a smooth paste. Add the egg whites, cream, lemon juice, dill and chives, and process briefly using the pulse. Season with salt, white pepper and nutmeg. Alternatively, chop the fish very finely by hand and mix with the other ingredients.

Preheat the oven to 180°C (350°F/Gas 4). Transfer half of the pike mixture to loaf tin. Cut the salmon into short, thin strips. Lay the salmon strips on top, all facing the same direction so the pâté will cut easily. Season with salt and white pepper and cover with the remaining pike mixture. Cover with foil and place in a roasting tin. Add boiling water until one-third of the loaf tin is immersed in water. You may find it easier to add the boiling water to the tin once the tin is in the oven.

Bake for 40–45 minutes or until firm to the touch. Remove tin from water and leave until cold. Refrigerate overnight. Place a large plate on top of the tin and invert both so that the terrine comes out onto the plate. Peel off the paper and serve in slices, garnished with salmon roe, cucumber, watercress and dill.

Fish substitution trout or carp

Process the pike to a fine paste in a food processor.

Transfer half of the pike mixture to the lined loaf tin.

Spread the remaining pike mixture over the salmon slices.

three ways with sauces

The makrut (kaffir lime) leaf and red curry sauce is a hot sauce that can also be used for shellfish, particularly prawns. It is popular in Thailand, where it is known as chuchi. The tropical herb and yoghurt dressing keeps the fish lovely and moist during cooking. It is suitable for any type of flat fish.

MAKRUT (KAFFIR LIME) LEAF AND RED CURRY SAUCE

Heat a wok or pan and add 80 ml (2$\frac{1}{2}$ fl oz/$\frac{1}{3}$ cup) oil. Heat oil until it begins to smoke, then add 2 crushed large garlic cloves and cook for 30 seconds, stirring all the time. Add 1–2 tablespoons red curry paste, to taste, and fry for 30 seconds. Add 270 ml (9$\frac{1}{2}$ fl oz) coconut milk and mix through. Add 80 ml (2$\frac{1}{2}$ fl oz/$\frac{1}{3}$ cup) fish sauce, 2 tablespoons sugar and 2 teaspoons lemon juice and heat through. Stir in 2 finely shredded makrut (kaffir lime) leaves and 2 tablespoons chopped coriander (cilantro) leaves. Spoon over cooked skinned fish fillets such as pomfret, sole or plaice, or prawns (shrimp). To prepare fish, put 80 ml (2$\frac{1}{2}$ fl oz/$\frac{1}{3}$ cup) oil in a large wok or frying pan until hot. Add 600 g (1 lb 5 oz) skinned fillets, in batches if necessary, and cook for 2–3 minutes, or until opaque. If cooking in batches, transfer the cooked fish to a plate and cover with foil while you cook the remainder. Serves 4.

TROPICAL HERB AND YOGHURT DRESSING

Grate a 4 cm (1$\frac{1}{2}$ inch) piece of fresh ginger. Mix together the ginger, 500 g (1 lb 2 oz) finely chopped onions, 50 g (1$\frac{3}{4}$ oz) chopped coriander (cilantro) leaves, 4–6 finely chopped green chillies, 1 tablespoon ground coriander, $\frac{1}{2}$ teaspoon ground turmeric and 250 ml (9 fl oz/1 cup) plain yoghurt. Stir in 1 tablespoon oil (if you would like a smoother paste, put everything through the blender for a few seconds). This dressing goes well with such fish as sole, hilsa, bony bream and pomfret. To use the dressing, put 1.5 kg (3 lb 5 oz) fish fillets, skin side down, in a shallow ovenproof dish. (If using hilsa or bream fillets, use tweezers to remove any small bones you can feel; they are notoriously bony fish.) Drizzle a little lime juice over the fillets, sprinkle with a pinch of salt, and rub salt in well. Cover and refrigerate for 1 hour. Preheat the oven to 180°C (350°F/Gas 4). Pour the yoghurt mixture over the fillets, making sure they are completely coated. Bake for 20 minutes, or until the fish flakes when tested with the point of a knife. Serves 6.

FRENCH BUTTER SAUCE

Put 400 ml (14 fl oz) fish stock, 80 ml (2$\frac{1}{2}$ fl oz/$\frac{1}{3}$ cup) dry white wine, 1 tablespoon white wine vinegar, 1 finely chopped French shallot, 1 bay leaf and 1 flat-leaf (Italian) parsley sprig in a small saucepan. Bring to the boil over high heat, then reduce the heat to medium and simmer until the liquid has reduced by two-thirds. Meanwhile, preheat the grill (broiler) to high and cover the grill tray with foil. Lightly brush the foil with 2 teaspoons oil. Cut 150 g (5$\frac{1}{2}$ oz) cold unsalted butter into small cubes, plate and refrigerate. Sieve the sauce, discarding the shallot and herbs. Return the sauce to the saucepan. Add 200 ml (7 fl oz) thick (double/heavy) cream and heat until reduced by half. Put 800 g (1 lb 12 oz) skinned fillets such as flathead, snapper, john dory or haddock on the grill tray. Drizzle with the juice of half a lemon and season with salt and freshly ground black pepper. Grill (broil) for 7–10 minutes, or until the fish is opaque and just cooked through. Meanwhile, finish the sauce; keeping the sauce simmering but not boiling, add the butter, cube by cube, to the sauce, whisking thoroughly after each addition. Stir in 2 tablespoons finely chopped flat-leaf (Italian) parsley and season with salt and black pepper. Serve the fish with some sauce drizzled over the top; pass any remaining sauce in a pitcher. Serves 4.

fish with makrut (kaffir lime) leaf and red curry sauce

Kedgeree

SERVES 4

This traditional English breakfast dish is based on an Indian recipe. When buying smoked fish, select thick pieces from the centre of the fillet. Bright yellow or orange smoked fish has been dyed; look for the paler, undyed variety, which has been smoked for longer and has a better flavour.

smoked haddock or cod	350 g (12 oz)
lemon	3 slices
bay leaf	1
milk	300 ml (10½ fl oz)
long-grain rice	175 g (6 oz/heaped ¾ cup)
butter	60 g (2¼ oz)
onion	1 small, finely chopped
mild curry powder	2 teaspoons
flat-leaf (Italian) parsley	1 tablespoon, finely chopped
eggs	3 hard-boiled, roughly chopped
thick (double/heavy) cream	170 ml (5½ fl oz/⅔ cup)
mango chutney	to serve

Put the smoked fish in a deep frying pan with the lemon slices and bay leaf, cover with the milk and simmer for 6 minutes, or until cooked through. Remove the fish with a slotted spoon and break into large flakes. Discard any bones.

Put the rice in a saucepan along with 350 ml (12 fl oz) water, bring to the boil, cover and cook for 10 minutes, or until just cooked — there should be steam holes in the rice. Drain any excess water and fluff up the rice with a fork.

Melt the butter in a frying pan over medium heat. Add the onion and cook for 3 minutes, or until soft. Add the curry powder and cook for another 2 minutes. Add the rice and carefully stir through, cooking for 2–3 minutes, or until it is heated through. Add the fish, parsley, eggs and cream and stir until heated through. Season well with freshly ground black pepper. Serve immediately with mango chutney.

Fish substitution smoked cod fillets

Chutney is usually understood in the West to mean a sweet, spicy, cooked preserve of sugar, vinegar, spices and fruit. However, this generally store-bought type is a world away from the original Indian version, which may be more of a paste, and is traditionally hand-ground on a stone. Fresh ingredients are used, such as ginger, chillies, onion, garlic, coriander, coconut, seed spices, or anything else considered piquant or refreshing. Commercially produced mango chutney uses underripe mangoes with such spices as chilli, ginger and cumin to make a mildly spicy relish that is the typical accompaniment for kedgeree, as well as for various curries.

Salmon coulibiac

Traditionally, this Russian pie would use a yeast dough rather than a flaky pastry dough. The filling almost always contains fish along with hard-boiled eggs, dill and parsley; this version adds mushrooms. Try to buy salmon fillets cut from the centre rather than the tail end of the fish.

basmati rice	60 g (2¼ oz/⅓ cup)
eggs	2 hard-boiled, chopped
dill	2 tablespoons, chopped
flat-leaf (Italian) parsley	2 tablespoons, chopped
thick (double/heavy) cream	60 ml (2 fl oz/¼ cup)
butter	60 g (2¼ oz)
onion	1, finely chopped
button mushrooms	200 g (7 oz), sliced
lemon juice	2 tablespoons
salmon fillet	500 g (1 lb 2 oz) centre-cut piece, skinned
frozen puff pastry	500 g (1 lb 2 oz) block, thawed
egg	1, lightly beaten

Cook rice in boiling salted water until just *al dente*, then drain and transfer to a bowl. When cooled slightly, add the chopped hard-boiled egg, dill and parsley, season with salt and freshly ground black pepper and stir in the cream.

Melt half the butter in a frying pan and add onion. Cook for 5 minutes, or until soft but not brown. Add mushrooms and cook for 5 minutes, or until soft. Add the lemon juice to the pan and stir to combine. Transfer the mixture to a bowl.

Melt the remaining butter in the same frying pan, add salmon fillet and cook for 2 minutes on each side to brown it. Transfer to a plate and allow to cool slightly.

Lightly grease a baking tray. Roll out half the pastry to a rectangle measuring 30 x 40 cm (12 x 16 inches) and place on the baking tray. Spread rice mixture onto the pastry, leaving a 3 cm (1¼ inch) border all the way around. Top with the piece of salmon and add mushroom mixture. Mould the layers to fit the shape of the salmon fillet.

Roll out the remaining pastry to approximately 33 x 43 cm (13 x 17 inches) and carefully place over the filling. Press the edges of the pastry together, trim the edges to a neat rectangle and crimp to seal. Decorate with shapes made from offcuts of pastry, if desired, then refrigerate for 30 minutes. Meanwhile, preheat the oven to 210°C (415°F/Gas 6–7). Brush pastry with the lightly beaten egg and make four slits in the top to allow the steam to escape. Bake for 15 minutes, then reduce the heat to 180°C (350°F/Gas 4) and bake for a further 15–20 minutes, or until the top is golden brown.

Fish substitution ocean trout, trout

Roll out half the pastry to a 30 x 40 cm (12 x 16 inch) rectangle.

Top the pastry with the rice mixture and the fish fillet.

Sardine ripiene

To make a sardine dish memorable, the fish must be really fresh; sardines, like mackerel, do not last long out of the water. Whole sardines will look neater, as you can just fold the fish in half. If you can only get fillets, try to get them with their tails on, as these will look more attractive.

sardines	8 medium, butterflied, heads removed, tails left on
olive oil	60 ml (2 fl oz/¼ cup)
onion	1 small, thinly sliced
fennel bulb	1, thinly sliced
pine nuts	50 g (1¾ oz/⅓ cup)
flat-leaf (Italian) parsley	4 tablespoons, roughly chopped
fresh breadcrumbs	20 g (¾ oz/¼ cup)
garlic	1 large clove, crushed
lemon juice	2 tablespoons
extra virgin olive oil	to serve
lemon wedges	to serve

Rinse the sardines in cold water and drain on paper towels. Leave in the refrigerator until needed.

Preheat the oven to 200°C (400°F/Gas 6). To prepare stuffing, heat the olive oil in a frying pan and add the onion, fennel and pine nuts. Cook over moderately high heat until soft and light brown, stirring frequently. Mix 1 tablespoon of parsley with 1 tablespoon of the breadcrumbs and set aside. Add the garlic and remaining breadcrumbs to the pan and cook for a few minutes more. Add the rest of the parsley, season and set aside. The stuffing mix can be made in advance and kept in the refrigerator but should be brought back to room temperature before cooking.

Drizzle a little olive oil in an ovenproof dish in which about 8 sardines fit in a single layer. Arrange the fish in the dish, skin side down, and season with salt and pepper. Spread the stuffing over the sardines and fold over to encase. If you are using fillets, spread half the fillets with stuffing, then place the other fillets on the top, skin side up, tail to tail like a sandwich. Season again and then sprinkle with parsley and breadcrumb mixture. Drizzle with the lemon juice and a little extra virgin olive oil.

Bake for 5–10 minutes, depending on the size of the sardines. If the filling is still warm, the sardines will cook more quickly. Serve immediately or at room temperature with lemon wedges.

To butterfly sardines yourself, first scale, gut and clean them.

The next step is to cut along the back then remove the head.

Finally, lift the backbone away from the flesh.

three ways with pâté

These recipes use different types of smoked fish. Smoked foods are first treated with either brine or dry salt, then smoked over smouldering sawdust. The wood used helps determine the flavour of the finished product. There are two methods of smoking. Cold smoking flavours the food without cooking it; such foods generally need to be cooked before they are eaten, smoked salmon being an exception. Hot smoking cooks the food while also imparting a delicious smoky flavour.

SMOKED TROUT PÂTÉ

Skin 2 whole smoked trout, remove the heads, then lift the flesh off the bones. Alternatively, use 4 skinned smoked trout fillets. Break the flesh into flakes and put in a bowl or food processor. Either mash the flesh with a fork or briefly process until it is broken up, but still with plenty of texture. Beat 200 g (7 oz) cream cheese with a wooden spoon until soft. Add the smoked trout flesh and mix together well. Stir in 2 tablespoons finely chopped dill and the juice of half a lemon. Season with salt, freshly ground black pepper and a pinch of cayenne pepper. Chill the pâté until you need it, but bring it to room temperature before serving. Serve with toasted slices of baguette, melba toast, or triangles of brown toast with the crusts removed. Provide extra lemon wedges to squeeze over. Serves 6.

SMOKED SALMON PÂTÉ

Put 2 tablespoons rinsed, dried and roughly chopped capers and 1 seeded and finely chopped small red chilli in a food processor. Add 100 g (3½ oz) smoked salmon (trimmings are fine) and blend for about 10 seconds. Add 185 g (6¼ oz) mascarpone cheese and blend until smooth. Add 3–4 tablespoons milk, depending on how thick pâté is, and blend again. Transfer to a bowl and then add 1 tablespoon finely chopped flat-leaf (Italian) parsley and 1–2 tablespoons lemon juice, to taste. Season with salt and freshly ground black pepper and refrigerate until needed. Serve with melba toast or triangles of brown toast with the crusts removed. Serves 4–6.

SMOKED MACKEREL PÂTÉ

Remove the skin from 225 g (8 oz) peppered smoked mackerel fillets (about 2 fillets). Put them in a bowl and mash with a fork. Add 80 g (2¾ oz) sour cream, 1 tablespoon creamed horseradish and 2 tablespoons lime juice. Mix everything together well, season with a little salt if needed, then refrigerate until ready to use. Serve with melba toast or triangles of brown toast with the crusts removed. This also makes a great sandwich filling with watercress. Serves 4–6.

smoked trout pâté

Caruru

SERVES 4

This rich and creamy Brazilian stew has an African influence. It is traditionally served with a spicy pepper and lemon sauce consisting of tabasco peppers, onions, garlic and lemon juice.

tomatoes	350 g (12 oz)
dried shrimps	1 tablespoon
oil	3 tablespoons
onion	1, chopped
green capsicum (pepper)	1 small, seeded and chopped
green chilli	1, finely chopped
garlic	3 cloves, crushed
crunchy peanut butter	3 tablespoons
coconut milk	400 ml (14 fl oz)
okra	100 g (3½ oz) small, topped and tailed
paprika	½ teaspoon
cod fillet	600 g (1 lb 5 oz), skinned
coriander (cilantro)	3 tablespoons chopped

Score a cross in the base of each tomato. Plunge into boiling water for 20 seconds, then drain and peel the skin away from the cross. Chop the tomatoes, discarding the cores and seeds.

Put the dried shrimps in a small bowl, cover with boiling water and leave to soak for 10 minutes, then drain.

Heat the oil in a deep-sided frying pan. Add onion and green capsicum and cook for 5 minutes, stirring occasionally. Add the chilli and garlic and cook for a further 2 minutes, stirring. Add the chopped tomato and its juices, peanut butter, coconut milk, okra, paprika and dried shrimp. Bring mixture to the boil, then reduce the heat to medium and simmer for 12–15 minutes, or until the okra are tender.

Meanwhile, cut the cod into large chunks. Add the fish to the pan, stir and simmer gently to cook. Test after 3 minutes; if the cod flakes easily, it is ready. Season and scatter the coriander over the top.

Fish substitution bream, bass, prawns

Note Dried shrimps are available from shops selling Asian or South American and Caribbean produce. You may need to soak the dried shrimp for more than 10 minutes if very hard.

Chop the peeled tomatoes, discarding the cores and seeds.

Cover the dried shrimps with boiling water and leave to soak.

Add the tomato, peanut butter, coconut milk, okra and prawns.

Redfish in corn husks with asparagus

SERVES 6

Corn husks are available ready prepared for making tamales. If preparing your own, cut off the base and points of the husks. Pour boiling water over the husks and let soak for several hours, or until pliable. Drain and dry them well before filling them. Or use baking paper or foil instead.

red capsicum dressing

red capsicum (pepper)	1
extra virgin olive oil	2 tablespoons
garlic	1 small clove, crushed
lemon juice	1 tablespoon
basil	1 tablespoon chopped
pine nuts	1 tablespoon
small black olives	100 g (3½ oz/½ cup)
redfish	6 small, scaled and gutted
lemon thyme	12 sprigs
lemon	1, sliced
garlic	2 cloves, sliced
corn husks	12 large
olive oil	for drizzling
fresh asparagus	350 g (12 oz/2 bunches), trimmed
lemon wedges	for serving

To make the red capsicum dressing, cut the capsicum into large pieces. Place, skin side up, under a hot grill (broiler) until the skin blackens and blisters. (Alternatively, hold the capsicum over the gas flame of your stove until the skin is blackened.) Put capsicum in a plastic bag, seal the bag, and allow capsicum to cool before peeling away the skin and finely dicing the flesh.

In a small bowl, whisk together the extra virgin olive oil, garlic, lemon juice and basil. Add the capsicum, pine nuts and olives.

Wash the fish and pat dry inside and out with paper towels. Fill each fish cavity with thyme, lemon and garlic, then place each fish in a corn husk. Drizzle with oil and sprinkle with freshly ground black pepper, then top each fish with another husk. Tie each end of the husks with string to enclose.

Preheat a barbecue flatplate or a coal fire to high. Put the parcels on flatplate or coals and cook for 6–8 minutes, or until the fish is cooked and flakes easily when tested with the point of a knife. Turn parcels once during the cooking. A few minutes after you have started cooking the fish, brush asparagus with oil and add to barbecue or coals. Cook, turning occasionally, for 3–4 minutes, or until tender. Pour dressing over the asparagus and serve with the fish. Discard husks before eating.

Fish substitution red mullet

Fill the cavity of each fish with thyme, lemon and garlic.

Place each fish in a corn husk, drizzle with oil and season.

Cook on a barbecue flatplate or over coals, turning once.

the perfect fish stock

A good home-made fish stock makes a huge difference to fish-based soups, sauces and stews and is the simplest of all stocks to make. It is also quick to make — in fact, too long a cooking time will produce a bitter stock. Fish stock is made by simmering together the uncooked fish bones and heads and/or the shells of crustaceans with water, vegetables and a few aromatics such as peppercorns and herbs. To make a decent amount of stock, quite a few bones are needed; the easiest way to get them is to ask the fishmonger for the bones left over after he or she fillets fish for you (or, fillet the fish yourself and retain the bones). Store the bones in the freezer until you have enough. It is important to avoid oily fish, such as herring and mackerel.

To make the fish stock, put about 1 kg (2 lb 4 oz) fish bones, heads and trimmings (but not any innards) and crustacean shells in a large saucepan. Add 1 roughly chopped onion, 1 thickly sliced carrot, a few peppercorns, 1 bay leaf and some parsley stalks (not the leaves) if you have any. Cover with about 2 litres (70 fl oz/8 cups) water and bring to the boil. Reduce to a simmer and then cook, uncovered, for 20 minutes, skimming off any scum that comes to the surface. Strain, then leave to cool. Refrigerate until needed, removing any fat that forms on the surface. Store in refrigerator for up to 3 days or freeze for up to 6 months.

If freezer space is limited, once the stock is strained, return it to a clean saucepan and boil vigorously until it is reduced by three-quarters to two-thirds. Leave to cool, then pour into ice-cube trays and freeze. Once frozen, the cubes can then be transferred to freezer bags. When using the concentrated stock cubes, remember to add water to the dish to return the stock to its original strength.

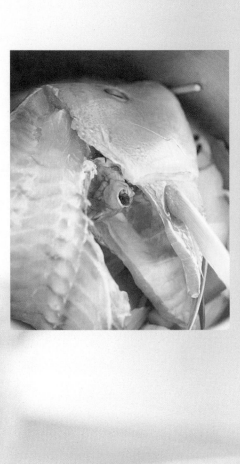

Russian fish pies with mushrooms

SERVES 4

Pies known as pirogi are very popular in Russia. They are usually large and rectangular, but this recipe makes individual crescent-shaped pies. The fillings may be savoury or sweet. Fish pirogi are traditionally made with sturgeon, but any firm white fish may be used.

pastry

plain (all-purpose) flour	300 g (10½ oz/2⅓ cups)
salt	a pinch
butter	175 g (6 oz), chilled and cubed
egg yolks	3 large
iced water	as needed

filling

long-grain white rice	50 g (1¾ oz)
firm white fish fillet	450 g (1 lb), skinned
butter	50 g (1¾ oz)
mushrooms	200 g (7 oz), sliced
sour cream	200 ml (7 fl oz)
lemon juice	1 tablespoon
flat-leaf (Italian) parsley	3 tablespoons, chopped

To make the pastry, sieve the flour with a generous pinch of salt into a large bowl. Rub the butter into the flour until fine crumbs form. Lightly beat 2 of the egg yolks and stir into the flour mixture with a little iced water. Mix together, adding more water if necessary to bring the dough together. Wrap the dough in plastic wrap and refrigerate for at least 30 minutes.

To make the filling, put rice in a small saucepan with 100 ml (3½ fl oz) boiling water and a pinch of salt. Bring to the boil, then reduce the heat to medium-low and cook, covered with a tight-fitting lid, for 15 minutes. Add a further 1–2 tablespoons boiling water if the rice begins to dry out. Allow to cool.

Chop the fish coarsely. Melt the butter in a large frying pan and when hot, add the mushrooms. Cook for 4–5 minutes, or until soft. Add fish and cook, stirring occasionally, for 4–5 minutes, or until the fish is opaque. Remove the pan from theat and stir in the cooked rice, sour cream, lemon juice and parsley. Season with salt and freshly ground black pepper and set aside until cold. Preheat the oven to 190°C (375°F/Gas 5).

Roll the pastry out on a floured work surface to a thickness of 3 mm (⅛ inch). Cut out 8 or 10 circles, each 12 cm (4½ inches) in diameter. Put a tablespoon of filling on each circle, leaving a border around the edges, and fold the pastry in half to form a crescent shape. Press the edges together to seal. Cut two slits in the top of each pie to allow steam to escape. Transfer the pies to a large oiled and floured baking tray.

Mix the remaining egg yolk with a teaspoon of water and use to brush the edges of the pastry. Fold the pastry in half, seal the parcel and brush the outside with the egg yolk. Make two small cuts in the top for steam holes. Bake in the preheated oven for 30–35 minutes, or until the pastry is golden.

Steamed snapper with Asian flavours

SERVES 2

There are various species of fish known as snappers in Caribbean, Pacific and Asian waters. Most make very fine eating. As they age, some species develop a distinctive bulge above the eyes. Lemon grass, coriander (cilantro) and ginger add a piquant asian touch to this dish.

whole snapper	1, weighing about 800 g (1 lb 12 oz), scaled, fins removed and gutted
lemon grass	3 stems
coriander (cilantro) leaves	a handful
fresh ginger	3 cm (1¼ inch) piece, peeled and cut into thin matchsticks
garlic	1 large clove, peeled and cut into thin slivers
soy sauce	2 tablespoons
oil	60 ml (2 fl oz/¼ cup)
fish sauce	1 tablespoon
red chilli	1 small, seeded and finely diced
stir-fried Asian greens	to serve

Score the fish with diagonal cuts on both sides. Cut each lemon grass stem into three and lightly squash each piece with the end of the handle of a large knife. Put half of the lemon grass in the middle of a large piece of foil and lay the fish on top. Put the remaining lemon grass and half the coriander inside the cavity of the fish.

Mix ginger, garlic, soy sauce, oil, fish sauce and chilli together in a bowl. Drizzle the mixture over the fish and scatter the remaining coriander leaves over.

Enclose the fish in the foil and place in a bamboo or metal steamer over a large saucepan of simmering water. Steam for 25 minutes, or until the flesh of the fish is opaque and white. Transfer the foil package to a large serving plate and open at the table. Serve the fish with stir-fried Asian greens.

Fish substitution coral trout, sea bass, red emperor

Fresh coriander (also known as cilantro) is thought to be the world's most commonly used herb. Every part can be used: roots, stems, leaves and seeds. Different cuisines favour different parts: the seeds figure highly in European cooking, the roots are pounded for use in Thai curry pastes and the fresh leaves are used liberally in Southeast Asian and Latin American cooking. From India to Indonesia, the seeds are a vital part of curry pastes and spice mixes. In most Asian cooking, coriander leaves and roots are a key component in fish and shellfish dishes, due to the herb's aromatic flavour and natural affinity with such ingredients as ginger, chillies, lemon grass and lime juice.

Otak-otak

These spicy fish cakes are seen in the markets of Singapore, cooking over hot coals or under a grill (broiler), and are a popular lunchtime snack. The parcels can be unwrapped and the steaming contents eaten immediately or chilled and eaten as a light snack when cold.

groper fillets	450 g (1 lb), skinned and boned
dried red chillies	2 small
banana leaf	14 pieces, measuring 12 x 16 cm (4$^{1}/_{2}$ x 6$^{1}/_{4}$ inches)
lemon grass	1 stem, cut into 3 pieces
onion	1 small, peeled and cut in half
garlic	1 large clove, peeled
ground turmeric	a generous pinch
palm sugar	1 teaspoon grated, or soft brown sugar
salt	a generous pinch
ground coriander	1 teaspoon
shrimp paste (balacan)	1 teaspoon
candlenuts, unsalted macadamia nuts or peanuts	1 tablespoon
mint	1 tablespoon chopped
coriander	1 tablespoon chopped
coconut milk	60 ml (2 fl oz/$^{1}/_{4}$ cup)

Cut the fillets into chunks. Cover and refrigerate until required.

Put the dried chillies in a small bowl, cover with boiling water and leave to soak. Put 14 cocktail sticks in a bowl and cover with cold water to soak.

If the banana leaf has been frozen it will be soft when thawed, but if fresh — and tough — it can be softened by blanching in boiling water for 1 minute, then draining and refreshing in cold water. Put the fish in a food processor and blend to a thick purée. Transfer to a mixing bowl. Drain chillies, removing any stalks still attached, and put in the processor with lemon grass, onion, garlic, turmeric, sugar, salt, ground coriander, shrimp paste, nuts, mint, coriander and coconut milk. Blend to a paste. Add the paste to the fish and mix to combine.

Drain the cocktail sticks. Put about 2 tablespoons of mixture in the middle of each piece of banana leaf. Enclose the filling by folding the shorter sides of the rectangle into the middle so that they overlap. Fold the 2 protruding ends in to make a small package. Secure the ends with a cocktail stick.

Preheat grill (broiler) or barbecue. Either put the parcels on a baking tray, smooth side up, and grill (broil), 10 cm (4 inches) from the element, for 5 minutes or put parcels on the barbecue, smooth side down, and cook for 5 minutes. The parcels are ready when banana leaf has lightly browned and parcels are hot in the middle (open them to check this). Eat warm or cold.

Fish substitution hapuka, blue warehou, halibut, haddock, snapper

If using fresh banana leaf, blanch first, then drain and refresh.

Wrap the filling in the banana leaf and secure with a cocktail stick.

Crispy fried fish with chilli and cucumber   SERVES 2

Deep-frying whole fish until golden and crisp is an Asian technique. Turning the fish is less tricky if you use special tools known as spiders; these have several metal segments that fan out, giving a large surface area and allowing you to manoeuvre a whole fish while keeping it intact.

whole pomfret	500 g (1 lb 2 oz), head intact, scaled and gutted
oil	60 ml (2 fl oz/¼ cup)
red Asian shallots	4, or 1 small onion, thinly sliced
garlic	1 clove, finely chopped
fresh ginger	1 teaspoon grated
red chillies	3 small, seeded and finely chopped
palm sugar	2 tablespoons grated, or soft brown sugar
tamarind purée	1 tablespoon
lime	zest and juice of 1
fish sauce	2 tablespoons
Lebanese (short) cucumber	1 large, peeled and cut into thin batons
oil	for deep-frying
coriander (cilantro) leaves	1 tablespoon chopped

Score diagonal cuts on both sides of the fish.

Heat the oil in a wok or sauté pan. When the oil is just beginning to smoke, add the shallots or onion and cook for 2 minutes, stirring, or until they are beginning to soften and colour. Add the garlic, ginger and chillies and cook for a further minute, or until lightly golden and crisp. Mix the sugar, tamarind, lime juice and fish sauce together and add to the sauce. Allow to bubble for 30 seconds, or until the sauce thickens slightly. Stir in the cucumber and remove from the heat. Transfer the sauce to a small saucepan and set aside.

Clean the wok or pan and add oil to a depth of 2.5 cm (1 inch). Heat to 180°C (350°F), or until a cube of white bread dropped into the oil browns in 15 seconds. Gently lower the fish into the oil and cook for 4–5 minutes, or until golden and crisp. Make sure the skin does not stick to the wok by moving the fish to and fro as you lower it in. Turn once during cooking, and spoon the hot oil over the fish as it cooks. Meanwhile, gently reheat the sauce. Drain the fish on paper towels. To serve, drizzle the sauce over the fish, then sprinkle with lime zest and coriander.

Fish substitution snapper, sea bass, bream

Once the oil begins to smoke, add the shallots.

Gently lower the fish into the oil and cook until golden and crisp.

Turn the fish once and spoon hot oil over it as it cooks.

Goan fish curry

SERVES 4

The food of Goa, on India's south-west coast, has been influenced by the Portuguese, who lived in the area for 500 years and introduced the now-ubiquitous chilli. Coconut, garlic, ginger and souring agents such as tamarind are also common in the region's cuisine.

cardamom pods	4
coriander seeds	1 teaspoon
yellow mustard seeds	2 teaspoons
shredded coconut	2 tablespoons
oil	60 ml (2 fl oz/¼ cup)
onion	1 large, chopped
garlic	2 cloves, finely chopped
green chillies	3 small, seeded and finely chopped
fresh ginger	1 tablespoon grated
ground turmeric	½ teaspoon
nutmeg	a pinch of freshly grated
cloves	4
tamarind purée	2 tablespoons
curry leaves	6
cinnamon sticks	2
coconut milk	800 ml (28 fl oz)
pomfret, plaice or sole fillets	600 g (1 lb 5 oz), skinned and cut into strips
small raw prawns (shrimp)	12, peeled and deveined

Lightly crush the cardamom pods until the pods split, then remove the seeds from the pods and put in a small frying pan with the coriander seeds. Dry-fry until fragrant and the seeds begin to jump. Remove from the heat and tip into a mortar and pestle or spice grinder. Grind the seeds to a powder.

Tip the mustard seeds into the frying pan with the coconut and toast together until the seeds begin to pop and the coconut turns light golden. Remove from the heat and set aside.

Heat the oil in a medium saucepan and add the onion. Cook for 4–5 minutes, or until starting to soften. Add garlic, chilli, ginger, turmeric and nutmeg and cook for a further minute. Tip in the ground spices, toasted coconut and mustard seeds, cloves, tamarind, curry leaves, cinnamon sticks and coconut milk. Stir well and heat to just below boiling point, then reduce the heat and simmer, uncovered, for 10 minutes, or until slightly thickened. Add the fish and the prawns and poach for 5 minutes, or until fish is opaque and the prawns are pale pink.

Cardamom is a sweet, aromatic spice, used in both sweet and savoury dishes. In Africa, it is added to coffee and spice mixes such as the Moroccan ras el hanout; Scandinavian cooks flavour cookies with its mild sweetness; and in India, the seeds are used whole or ground to flavour curries, rice dishes and milk desserts. In Goan cuisine, cardamom is most often seen in the spicy fish dishes that are at the heart of the region's cooking. During its colonial period, Goa was an important trading stop for Portugal, and cardamom was one of its most valuable commodities. Buy the seeds still in the pod, as they lose their flavour quickly once rid of the protective shell.

Baked coral trout and fennel

SERVES 2

Fennel makes a wonderfully aromatic complement for fish. The fine, feathery leaves can be snipped like a herb and used to flavour fish, and the bulb may may be eaten raw like celery, or braised or sautéed then added to recipes. All parts have a delicate flavour similar to aniseed.

florence fennel bulbs	2 small, about 270 g (9½ oz) each
butter	2 tablespoons
olive oil	2 tablespoons
onion	1, chopped
garlic	1 clove, crushed
coral trout	1, gutted and scaled (about 800 g–1 kg/ 1 lb 12 oz–2 lb 4 oz after cleaning)
extra virgin olive oil	for brushing
lemon	1, quartered
oregano	2 teaspoons chopped
lemon wedges	to serve

Preheat the oven to 190°C (375°F/Gas 5) and grease a large shallow ovenproof dish. Finely slice the fennel bulbs, reserving the green fronds.

Heat the butter and olive oil in a large frying pan and gently cook the fennel, onion and garlic for 12–15 minutes, or until softened but not browned. Season with salt and pepper.

Stuff the fish with a heaped tablespoon of the cooked fennel mixture and a quarter of the fennel fronds. Brush with extra virgin olive oil, squeeze the lemon over and season well.

Put the remaining fennel fronds and cooked fennel into the dish and sprinkle with half of the oregano. Arrange the fish on top of the fennel. Sprinkle the remaining oregano over the fish and cover the dish loosely with foil. Bake for 25 minutes, or until just cooked through. Serve with lemon wedges and topped with some of the cooked fennel mixture.

Fish substitution snapper

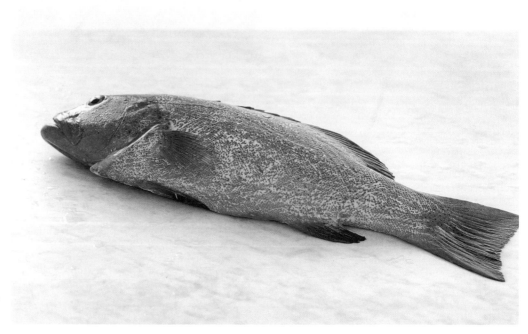

Coral trout (also known as coral cod) is not related to true trouts or cods, but is instead a species of grouper. Its coloration is striking; the body is a pink-orange and the spots blue. These fish occur in Indo-Pacific waters and, like all groupers, can grow to enormous sizes, but it is the smaller specimens that make the best eating. The firm, flaky flesh lends itself well to a variety of cooking methods.

three ways with flat fish

Flat fish include plaice, flounder, sole, halibut, dab and turbot. Strictly speaking, the term applies to one zoological order of mostly ambush-feeding fish that lie on their sides on the sea floor, and whose heads have become twisted around so that both eyes are now on the top side. However, some narrow fish that swim around upright, such as john dory and pomfret, are also sometimes called flat fish, and can be substituted for true flat fish.

JOHN DORY WITH PEA PURÉE

Chop 1 onion and finely chop 2 rindless bacon slices (total weight about 85 g/3 oz). Heat 1 tablespoon olive oil in a medium saucepan and fry the onion and bacon for 4–5 minutes. Stir in 300 g (10$\frac{1}{2}$ oz) frozen peas, 185 ml (6 fl oz/$\frac{3}{4}$ cup) vegetable or chicken stock and 1 mint sprig. Bring to the boil, then simmer for about 10 minutes. Allow to cool slightly, discard mint sprig and transfer to a blender or food processor. Process until roughly puréed; the mixture should not be smooth. Return to the clean saucepan, stir in 2 tablespoons thick (double/heavy) cream, season and gently reheat. Meanwhile, wash and pat dry four 175 g (6 oz) skinned john dory fillets. Dust lightly in seasoned flour and fry, two at a time if necessary, in 30 g (1 oz) melted butter for about 3 minutes. Turn and then cook for 1–2 minutes on the other side, or until golden brown. Serve the fillets on a bed of pea purée. Serves 4.

TURBOT WITH CREAMY MUSHROOM SAUCE

Preheat the oven to 130°C (250°F/Gas 1) and warm 4 plates. Put 1 tablespoon oil and a small knob of butter in a large frying pan over high heat. Once the butter is bubbling, add four 175 g (6 oz) skinned fillets of turbot or other flat fish (you may need to add them two at a time). Leave for 3 minutes, then turn over and cook for 1–2 minutes, or until just cooked through. Transfer the fillets to the oven to keep warm. Add another tablespoon of oil to the pan and add 125 g (4$\frac{1}{2}$ oz) finely chopped Swiss brown mushrooms. Fry for 2 minutes, or until softened. Add 250 ml (9 fl oz/1 cup) thick (double/heavy) cream. Cook until heated through. Remove from the heat, stir in 2 tablespoons chopped chives and season with salt and freshly ground black pepper. Spoon over the fish and serve immediately, accompanied by lemon wedges. Serves 4.

WARM TURBOT SALAD WITH SHAVED FENNEL

Steam four 175 g (6 oz) skinned turbot fillets for about 5 minutes over simmering water, until just cooked. Set aside to cool slightly. Meanwhile, combine 80 ml (2$\frac{1}{2}$ fl oz/$\frac{1}{3}$ cup) olive oil and 2 tablespoons sherry vinegar. Trim and very thinly slice 1 baby fennel and put in a bowl with half the oil and vinegar. Toss together. Arrange 125 g (4$\frac{1}{2}$ oz) mixed salad leaves on four serving plates and top with the fennel and turbot. Scatter over a handful of mint leaves and drizzle over the remaining dressing. Serves 4.

john dory with pea purée

Sole à la meunière

Of the many species of sole, the most prized is the species solea solea. In Britain, it is often called dover sole, to distinguish it from the unrelated lemon sole. The simple lemon and butter sauce of this classic recipe complements the fish's firm white flesh and delicate flavour.

whole dover sole	4, gutted and dark skin removed
plain (all-purpose) flour	30 g (1 oz/¼ cup)
clarified butter	200 g (7 oz) (see note)
lemon juice	2 tablespoons
flat-leaf (Italian) parsley	4 tablespoons, chopped
lemon wedges and steamed greens	to serve

Pat the fish dry with paper towels. Cut away the fine bones and frill of skin from around the edge of the fish, remove the heads if you like, dust lightly with the flour and season with salt and freshly ground white pepper. Heat 150 g (5½ oz) of the butter in a frying pan large enough to fit all 4 fish, or cook the fish in 2 batches, using 75 g (2¾ oz) butter for each batch.

Put fish in the pan, skinned side up, and cook for 4 minutes, or until golden. Carefully turn over and then cook for a further 4 minutes, or until the fish is cooked through (the flesh will feel firm when done). Put fish on warm plates, drizzle with the lemon juice and sprinkle with the parsley. Add the remaining butter to the pan and heat until it browns, but do not let it get too brown or the sauce will taste burnt. Pour over the fish (it will foam as it mixes with the lemon juice) and serve with lemon wedges and steamed greens.

Fish substitution sole fillets

Note Clarified butter has a higher burning point than other butters because it doesn't contain any milk solids. To clarify butter, gently heat unsalted butter in a saucepan until liquid; do not stir. Leave until white milk solids settle to the bottom. Use a spoon to skim off any foam, then strain off the golden liquid, leaving white solids behind. Refrigerate the liquid.

Cut away the fine bones and frill of skin from the edge of the fish.

Lightly dust the fish with the seasoned flour.

Put the fish in the pan, skinned side up, and cook until golden.

Escabeche

SERVES 2

Escabeche is a way of preserving fish. The fish is first fried and then marinated overnight in a pickling solution. Originally Spanish, the recipe has spread to many other places. This recipe uses cinnamon, nutmeg and citrus juices, flavours that are often found in South African dishes.

sea bass or snoek fillet	450 g (1 lb), skinned
cod or barracuda fillet	450 g (1 lb), skinned
plain (all-purpose) flour	100 g (3½ oz)
vegetable oil	125 ml (4 fl oz/½ cup)
onion	1 medium, finely sliced into rings
garlic	1 large clove, finely chopped
white wine vinegar	200 ml (7 fl oz)
orange juice	2 tablespoons
lemon juice	2 tablespoons
orange zest	2 teaspoons
lemon zest	2 teaspoons
caster (superfine) sugar	2 tablespoons
ground cinnamon	2 teaspoons
ground nutmeg	2 teaspoons
turmeric	¼ teaspoon
paprika	¼ teaspoon

Cut fish fillets into strips measuring approximately 12 x 3 cm (4½ x 1¼ inches). Put the flour onto a plate and season with salt and pepper. Dip the fish in the seasoned flour.

Heat 3 tablespoons of the oil in a frying pan until hot and cook fish for 2 minutes on each side, or until lightly golden and crisp. You will need to cook in batches, so add another tablespoon of oil if necessary. Drain cooked fish on crumpled paper towels, then arrange in a single layer on a serving dish.

Wipe out pan and add remaining oil. When hot, add the onion and cook, stirring, over a low heat for 4–5 minutes, or until soft. Add the garlic and cook, stirring, for 2 minutes. Stir in vinegar, juices, zests, sugar, cinnamon, nutmeg, turmeric, paprika and 100 ml (3½ fl oz) water. Bring to the boil, simmer for 5 minutes, then pour over fish. Allow to cool, then cover and refrigerate overnight. Once cooked and marinated, the fish will keep for up to a week in the refrigerator. Eat at room temperature.

Fish substitution snapper, halibut, bream

Citrus zest – the thin, coloured outer layer of the rind – contains aromatic essential oils, which are rich in flavour. These oils release their flavour most readily when combined with fats, which is why citrus zests are often creamed with butter and sugar in baked good such as cakes and biscuits (cookies). Zests can also be infused in warm liquids or syrups to flavour them, and the liquid then added to the recipe. The zest can be grated, removed in fine scrolls with a special tool called a zester, or pared off in wider strips with a vegetable peeler and then sliced more finely if desired. Unless the recipe directs otherwise, use the zest only, not the white pith beneath, which is bitter.

Cullen skink

This Scottish soup traditionally includes Finnan haddock, or 'Finnan haddie', the famous smoked haddock from the village of Findon, near Aberdeen. The smoked fish gives the soup a delicious depth of flavour and the thick texture makes it a robust winter warmer.

smoked haddock (preferably Finnan haddock)	600 g (1 lb 5 oz)
milk	1.3 litres (45 fl oz)
butter	25 g (1 oz)
smoked streaky bacon	100 g (3½ oz), diced
onion	1 large, chopped
waxy potatoes	500 g (1 lb 2 oz), peeled and cut into small chunks
cream (whipping)	60 ml (2 fl oz/¼ cup)
chives	3 tablespoons, chopped

Put the haddock in a sauté pan or deep frying pan and pour the milk over the top. Bring the liquid to the boil, then reduce to a simmer, cover and poach gently for 10 minutes. When ready, the fish should be flaky when tested with the point of a sharp knife. Drain, reserving the milk. Flake the haddock into small pieces, discarding any skin and bones. Set aside.

Meanwhile, melt the butter in a large saucepan and when foaming, add the bacon and onion. Cook on a medium–low heat for 10 minutes, or until the onion has softened and is translucent. Add the potatoes and the reserved milk. Bring to the boil and simmer, covered, for 15–20 minutes, or until the potatoes are cooked. Stir in the haddock and cream, season to taste with salt and pepper, and bring back to a gentle simmer. Sprinkle the chopped chives over the top before serving.

Fish substitution smoked cod

Put the haddock in the pan and cover it with the milk.

Test the fish with the point of a knife to see if it is cooked.

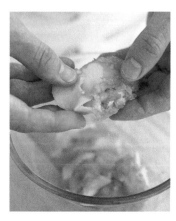

Break the cooked fish into flakes, discarding the skin and bones.

Hot and sour fish stew

SERVES 4

Combinations of hot and sour ingredients — such as fresh chillies, garlic, sugar, lime juice and vinegar or tamarind — are often found in Southeast Asian cooking.

spice paste	
lemon grass	2 stems, white part only, cut into three pieces
ground turmeric	1 teaspoon
fresh galangal or ginger	a small knob
red chillies	3 small
garlic	1 large clove, peeled
red Asian shallots	4, peeled
shrimp paste	1 teaspoon
oil	60 ml (2 fl oz/¼ cup)
red capsicum (pepper)	½ small, thinly sliced into strips
tamarind purée or lemon juice	3 tablespoons
fish sauce	1 tablespoon
palm sugar	2 teaspoons grated, or soft brown sugar
canned sliced bamboo shoots	225 g (8 oz), drained
pomfret fillets	500 g (1 lb 2 oz) skinned, cut into bite-sized pieces
coriander (cilantro) leaves	2 tablespoons, chopped
mint	1 tablespoon, chopped
steamed rice	to serve

To make the spice paste, put all the ingredients in a food processor and process to a paste. Alternatively, finely chop all the ingredients and mix together by hand.

Heat the oil in a large saucepan and add the spice paste. Cook for 10 minutes, stirring. Add capsicum strips and cook for a further minute. Add 750 ml (26 fl oz/3 cups) water, the tamarind, fish sauce, sugar and ½ teaspoon salt and then bring to the boil. Reduce heat to low and simmer for 5 minutes, add the bamboo shoots and fish pieces and poach the fish gently for 3–4 minutes, or until opaque. Stir in coriander and mint and serve over plenty of steamed rice.

Fish substitution lemon sole (lemon fish), plaice, sea bass, john dory

Finely process the spice paste ingredients in a food processor.

Add the bamboo shoots and fish pieces to the mixture.

Roasted blue-eye cod with lentil salad   SERVES 4

Blue-eye cod is commonly found in the cold seas off the south island of New Zealand, where it is available and eaten all year. Its firm white flesh is highly regarded and its thickness suits roasting at a high temperature.

puy lentils	200 g (7 oz)
pine nuts	50 g (1¾ oz/⅓ cup)
olive oil	100 ml (3½ fl oz)
red capsicum (pepper)	1, seeded and cut into thin strips
orange capsicum (pepper)	1, seeded and cut into thin strips
blue-eye cod	4 thick fillets, skinned
lemon juice	1 tablespoon
red onion	1 small, finely diced
balsamic vinegar	60 ml (2 fl oz/¼ cup)
basil	2 tablespoons, shredded

Put the lentils in a saucepan, cover with water and bring to the boil over high heat. Boil for 5 minutes, then reduce the heat to medium and continue to cook, uncovered, for 15–20 minutes, or until lentils are tender. You may need to top up lentils with boiling water as they cook. Drain and rinse under warm water.

Meanwhile, preheat the oven to 220°C (425°F/Gas 7). Place the pine nuts in a frying pan and toast over a low to medium heat until golden brown, shaking now and then. Transfer to a plate.

Heat 1 tablespoon of the olive oil in the frying pan and when hot, add the strips of capsicum. Cook for 5–7 minutes over medium heat, stirring now and then, or until tender when tested with the point of a small knife. Remove from the heat.

Put the fish in a roasting tin, brush each fillet with 2 teaspoons olive oil and drizzle the lemon juice over the top. Season with salt and pepper. Roast for 15–20 minutes in the preheated oven or until the fish is just opaque inside.

While the fish is cooking, in a bowl mix together the cooked lentils, peppers, toasted pine nuts, red onion, balsamic vinegar, basil and remaining olive oil. Season with salt and pepper. Serve each person a piece of cod topped with lentil salad.

Fish substitution thick snapper fillets, cod, haddock, ling

three ways with marinades

On hot days, or when long marinating times are called for, marinate foods in the refrigerator, but remember that flavours will take longer to penetrate the flesh when the ingredients are cold. Avoid brushing marinade onto food right at the end of the cooking time; allow it to cook on the food for about 5 minutes to kill any harmful pathogens. For the same reason, if you wish to serve leftover marinade as a sauce, boil it beforehand for at least 5 minutes.

BLACKENED CAJUN MARINADE

Combine 2 tablespoons cajun spice mix and 2 teaspoons sweet paprika with 2 tablespoons olive oil, 1 tablespoon lemon juice, 2 crushed garlic cloves and 1 tablespoon finely chopped flat-leaf (Italian) parsley. Pour over 4 large skinned fish fillets such as snapper, blue-eye, ling, warehou or mahi mahi, about 2 cm (³/₄ inch) thick and weighing about 200 g (7 oz) each. Use your fingers to rub the spice mix evenly over the fillets and leave to marinate in the refrigerator for 1–1¹/₂ hours. Melt 35 g (1¹/₄ oz) unsalted butter in a large pan over high heat and cook the fillets, two at a time, for 1–2 minutes on the first side. Turn over and cook for another few minutes, or until the fish is cooked and flakes easily. The surface should be well charred on each side. Serve with lemon halves — the lemons can be served lightly charred too if you like. The marinade makes enough for 4 fillets.

FISH TIKKA MARINADE

Mix together 250 g (9 oz/1 cup) Greek-style yoghurt, 2 finely chopped red Asian shallots, 1 tablespoon grated fresh ginger, 2 crushed garlic cloves, 2 tablespoons lemon juice, 1 teaspoon ground coriander, 1 tablespoon garam masala, 1 teaspoon paprika, 1 teaspoon chilli powder, 2 tablespoons tomato paste (concentrated purée) and 1 teaspoon salt in a shallow non-metallic dish that is long enough and deep enough to fit your fish. To use, brush the marinade over 4 skinned fish fillets (total weight about 500 g/1 lb 2 oz) such as sea bream, snapper, grouper, orange roughy or sea bass. Cover and leave to marinate in the refrigerator for at least 1 hour. The fish can be cooked in the oven, under the grill (broiler) or on a chargrill pan or barbecue flatplate. Cook for about 5 minutes, or until the fish is firm and opaque. Mix together 2 tablespoons chopped coriander (cilantro) leaves, 1 peeled and diced Lebanese (short) cucumber and 250 g (9 oz/1 cup) Greek-style yoghurt. Serve alongside the fish, with cooked vegetables such as onion and capsicum and lemon wedges to squeeze over. The marinade makes enough for 4 fillets.

SPICY ASIAN MARINADE

Cut the bottom 10 cm (4 inches) from a stalk of lemon grass and remove and discard its outer layers. Finely chop the rest of the stalk. Discard the leafy part of the lemon grass. Finely grate a 5 cm (2 inch) piece of fresh ginger and put in a bowl with the lemon grass, 1 seeded and finely chopped red chilli, 1 tablespoon fish sauce, 2 tablespoons lime juice, 2 tablespoons vegetable oil and 2 tablespoons chopped coriander (cilantro) leaves. Mix well. Arrange 750 g (1 lb 10 oz) fish strips or 4 x 175 g (6 oz) fillets in a shallow dish and pour over the marinade. Leave for 1–1¹/₂ hours, then remove the fish from the marinade and either stir-fry, if using strips, or grill (broil) or steam fillets. This marinade is suitable for flounder, sole or other flat fish. The marinade makes enough for 4 fillets.

fish with blackened cajun marinade

Whole sole simmered in sake and soy

SERVES 4

In Japan, ingredients are frequently simmered in flavoured cooking liquid and such recipes are called nimono. In this recipe, whole fish are gently simmered in a mixture of stock, sake, soy sauce, sugar and mirin. Serve with rice or noodles.

bonito-flavoured soup stock	½ sachet
caster (superfine) sugar	2 tablespoons
sake	80 ml (2½ fl oz/⅓ cup)
mirin	60 ml (2 fl oz/¼ cup)
Japanese soy sauce	80 ml (2½ fl oz/⅓ cup)
whole sole	2, each weighing 275–300 g (9¾–10½ oz), scaled and gutted
French beans	100 g (3½ oz), cut into 3 cm (1¼ inch) pieces
broccoli	100 g (3½ oz), cut into small florets

Put the soup stock in a large frying pan and add 500 ml (17 fl oz/2 cups) boiling water. Stir to combine and add the sugar, sake, mirin and soy sauce. Bring the mixture back to the boil and then reduce to a very gentle simmer.

Make a couple of diagonal slashes on the top side of each fish to ensure even cooking. Put the fish in the liquid, skin side up, and cover. Simmer for 5–6 minutes, or until the fish is opaque and cooked. Turn the fish over halfway through the cooking time. You may need to cook each fish separately, depending on the size of your pan.

Meanwhile, blanch the beans and broccoli in boiling water until just tender, drain and set aside.

A minute or so before the end of the cooking time, add the beans and broccoli to the simmering liquid. Serve each fish with a little cooking liquid spooned over it, accompanied by the vegetables.

Fish substitution plaice, flounder

Simmer the fish until it is opaque and cooked through.

Blanch the beans and broccoli in boiling water, then drain.

Kokoda

SERVES 6

In this refreshing fish salad from Fiji, raw fish is marinated in lime juice, which reacts with the protein in the flesh to 'cook' the fish. Only the freshest of fish are suitable for this recipe.

flounder	450 g (1 lb), skinned
lime juice	125 ml (4 fl oz/½ cup)
vine-ripened tomatoes	2
coconut milk	125 ml (4 fl oz/½ cup)
red chilli	1 small, seeded and finely chopped
French shallots	2, thinly sliced
garlic	1 clove, crushed
red capsicum (pepper)	1 small, diced

Cut the fish into small cubes and put in a non-metallic bowl. Add the lime juice and a generous pinch of salt and mix with a non-metallic spoon. Cover and leave to marinate in the refrigerator for at least 4 hours. Stir the fish every hour or so. You can leave the fish to marinate overnight if you prefer.

When the fish is ready, prepare the other ingredients. Score a cross in the base of each tomato. Put into boiling water for 20 seconds, then plunge into cold water. Drain and peel the skin away from the cross. Dice the tomatoes, discarding the cores and seeds.

Mix the tomatoes with the coconut milk, chilli, shallots, garlic and red capsicum. Drain the fish and combine with the coconut mixture. Taste to check the seasoning, adding more salt if necessary. Eat immediately or chill until required.

Fish substitution sole, plaice or any delicate white fish

Along with salt, smoke and vinegar, lime juice has been used for centuries to preserve food. The acid in the juice causes the protein in seafood to 'denature', that is, change chemically and physically, which stops biological activity and hence preserves the food. 'Cooking' fish in this way has been used around the world, and various Pacific Islands have similar recipes to the Fijian kokoda, all of which feature lime or lemon juice, coconut milk and white-fleshed fish. Take care when marinating fish, however, as fish is tenderized only, not cooked, so it must be of good enough quality to be served raw. For an authentic touch, serve the salad in coconut half-shells.

three ways with curry

Typical curry spices are turmeric, coriander, cumin, cloves, cardamom, ginger, tamarind, chilli, fennel, mustard seeds, cinnamon and fenugreek. Traditionally, spice mixtures for curries were stone-ground by hand and were made fresh each day. Once ground, spices quickly lose their flavour and aroma, so it is best to buy whole spices and grind them yourself. Alternatively, buy one of the many good-quality commercial curry pastes or powders that are now available.

INDIAN FISH CURRY

Put 2 tablespoons olive oil in a frying pan and add 2 finely chopped onions. Gently fry over low heat for 10 minutes. Finely grate a 5 cm (2 inch) piece of fresh ginger and add to the pan with 2 crushed garlic cloves. Cook for 3 minutes. Increase the heat to medium, then add 2 tablespoons Madras (hot) curry paste and fry for a further 2 minutes. Add 2 teaspoons ground coriander and cook for 2 minutes. Add 400 ml (14 fl oz) coconut milk, $1\frac{1}{2}$ tablespoons lime juice and bring to a simmer. Add 750 g (1 lb 10 oz) skinned fish pieces such as ling, cover and simmer for 8 minutes. Serve over rice, scattered with chopped coriander (cilantro), if liked. Serves 4.

FISH CURRY WITH COCONUT AND CHILLI

Mix together 100 g ($3\frac{1}{2}$ oz) finely chopped creamed coconut, 2 crushed garlic cloves, 3 seeded and finely chopped small green chilies, $\frac{1}{2}$ teaspoon each of ground turmeric, ground cloves, ground cinnamon and ground cayenne pepper, 1 tablespoon tamarind purée and 125 ml (4 fl oz/$\frac{1}{2}$ cup) oil. Put 800 g (1 lb 12 oz) skinned fish fillets such as pomfret, plaice or sole in a shallow dish and spoon the marinade over. Turn fish over, cover and set aside in the refrigerator for 30 minutes. Heat 30 ml (1 fl oz) oil in a large frying pan and when hot, add the fish, reserving any remaining marinade. Cook the fillets, in batches if necessary, for 1 minute on each side. When cooked, and with all the fish in the pan, reduce heat to low and add the reserved marinade and 200 ml (7 fl oz) coconut milk. Season with salt, cover and gently cook the fish for 3–5 minutes, or until cooked. Scatter 2 tablespoons chopped coriander (cilantro) leaves over the top and serve immediately. Serves 4.

FISH WITH CURRY SAUCE

Heat 2 tablespoons oil in a wok or sauté pan until hot. Add 600 g (1 lb 5 oz) skinned fish fillets such as pomfret, sole, plaice or blue eye — prawns (shrimp) are also good — to the wok or pan, adding them in batches if necessary. Cook for 2–3 minutes, or until opaque. Transfer to a plate and cover with foil. Wipe out the inside of the wok or pan and add another 2 tablespoons oil. Heat until hot, then add 2 crushed large garlic cloves and 90 g (3 oz/$\frac{1}{3}$ cup) red curry paste and fry for 30 seconds. Add 270 ml ($9\frac{1}{2}$ fl oz) coconut milk, 80 ml ($2\frac{1}{2}$ fl oz/$\frac{1}{3}$ cup) fish sauce, 2 tablespoons sugar and 2 teaspoons lemon juice and heat through. Stir in 2 teaspoons shredded makrut (kaffir lime) leaves and 2 tablespoons chopped coriander (cilantro) leaves and spoon the curry sauce over the fish. Garnish with a few extra coriander leaves. Serves 4.

indian fish curry

Skate with black butter

SERVES 4

This is considered by many as the classic way in which to prepare skate. Black or brown butter (beurre noire and beurre noisette) has accompanied French dishes for hundreds of years and in this recipe works wonderfully well with the sweet flavour of the skate.

court bouillon

white wine	250 ml (9 fl oz/1 cup)
onion	1, sliced
carrot	1, sliced
bay leaf	1
black peppercorns	4
skate wings	4 x 250 g (9 oz), skinned
capers	1 tablespoon
unsalted butter	100 g (3½ oz)
flat-leaf (Italian) parsley	1 tablespoon, chopped

To make the court bouillon, put the wine, onion, carrot, bay leaf, peppercorns and 1 litre (35 fl oz/4 cups) water into a large frying pan. Bring to the boil and simmer for 20 minutes. Strain the court bouillon and return liquid to the cleaned frying pan.

Add the skate, making sure that it is completely covered with the liquid, and simmer for 5–10 minutes (depending on the thickness of the wing), or until the flesh is opaque and flakes when tested with the point of a knife. Lift out the fish, drain, cover and keep warm until ready to serve.

Rinse, squeeze dry and chop the capers. Heat the butter in a frying pan and cook over moderate heat for about 2 minutes or until it turns brown to make a beurre noisette. Do not let it get too brown or it will taste burnt. Remove from the heat and stir in parsley and capers. Season with salt and black pepper. Pour the sauce over fish and serve immediately with steamed cubed potatoes and lemon wedges.

Fish substitution fillets of flat fish, such as sole, plaice or flounder, or snapper or perch

Simmer the skate until it is opaque and flakes when tested.

Rinse, squeeze dry and chop the capers.

Cook the butter over moderate heat until it is golden brown.

the perfect steamed fish

Steaming is a very gentle way to cook fish. If done properly, it is a wonderful way to retain the natural moistness, flavour, texture and shape of the fish. Steaming does not have to mean boring, bland-tasting fish, as it often did in the past, but — and this is true of any fish recipe — it does depend on the freshest of fish being used. Steamed fish is particularly common in Asian cuisine.

Most fish can be successfully steamed, although oily fish, such as tuna and mackerel, are best avoided. A multitude of flavourings can be added to the fish while it is cooking, but take care not to overwhelm the natural flavour of the fish. For delicately flavoured fish such as turbot and sea bass, just a sprig or two or herbs will suffice. However, for milder-tasting fish, try adding larger quantities of herbs, chillies, spices or sauces for an extra flavour boost.

Asian bamboo steamers are ideal, but must be washed and thoroughly dried after use to remove any fishy smell. Metal steamers are also suitable. Put 6–8 cm (2–3 inches) water into a saucepan and bring to a simmer. Put a plate, or a circle of baking paper that has been pricked with a skewer, in the steamer. Pile the plate or paper with any aromatics to be used and sit the fish on top, topping the fish with additional aromatics if liked. Cover with a lid and steam until the fish is just cooked through. For thin fillets, this can be as little 4–5 minutes; thicker fillets (around 450 g/1 lb) may take up to 8 or 10 minutes. Make sure the simmering water does not come into contact with the fish at any point. Be careful not to overcook the fish; it should be only just cooked through. White fish turns opaque when cooked, so check if the fish is cooked by piercing with a knife to see if the middle is also opaque. Any liquid on the plate can be drizzled over the fish when serving.

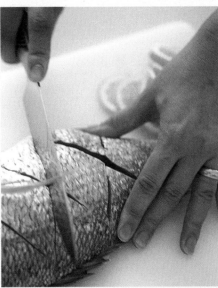

Barbecued garfish with pesto

SERVES 4

Garfish are quick and easy to cook on the barbecue or under the grill (broiler). They are usually sold whole as fresh fish or butterfly fillets and have a lovely sweet and tasty flesh. They can be quite bony, so bone them carefully.

garfish	8, scaled, boned and butterflied
olive oil	250 ml (9 fl oz/1 cup)
rosemary	1 tablespoon chopped
thyme	1 tablespoon chopped
butternut pumpkin (squash)	700 g (1 lb 9 oz), peeled
red onions	2 small

pesto
flat-leaf (Italian) parsley	30 g (1 oz/1 cup)
garlic	2 cloves, peeled
macadamia nuts	30 g (1 oz)
parmesan cheese	90 g (3 oz), grated
olive oil	150 ml (5 fl oz)

Pat the garfish dry and place in a non-metallic container. Season the fish on both sides with salt and pepper. Mix the oil with the rosemary and thyme and drizzle over the fish. Leave to marinate for an hour or so or until you are ready to cook.

Meanwhile, cut the butternut pumpkin into even-sized shapes measuring approximately 6 x 5 x 1 cm (2½ x 2 x ½ inch). Slice the onions thickly.

To make the pesto, place all the ingredients in a food processor and whizz to a paste. Alternatively, finely chop all ingredients by hand and mix. Season to taste.

Preheat a barbecue grill or hotplate to medium heat. Barbecue vegetables and fish on the grill or hotplate for 2–3 minutes on each side, brushing regularly with the remaining herb oil. You will need a wide spatula to turn the pumpkin on the barbecue grill. Serve the fish atop a few pumpkin slices and some of the red onion. Put a generous spoonful of pesto on top.

Fish substitution whiting, sardines, mackerel

To butterfly garfish, first scale, gut and clean them.

Remove the head and open out the fish, pressing it flat.

Lift out the bones; they should come away in one piece.

shellfish

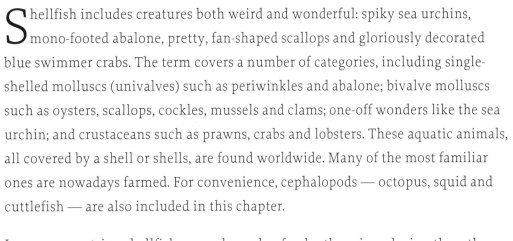

Shellfish includes creatures both weird and wonderful: spiky sea urchins, mono-footed abalone, pretty, fan-shaped scallops and gloriously decorated blue swimmer crabs. The term covers a number of categories, including single-shelled molluscs (univalves) such as periwinkles and abalone; bivalve molluscs such as oysters, scallops, cockles, mussels and clams; one-off wonders like the sea urchin; and crustaceans such as prawns, crabs and lobsters. These aquatic animals, all covered by a shell or shells, are found worldwide. Many of the most familiar ones are nowadays farmed. For convenience, cephalopods — octopus, squid and cuttlefish — are also included in this chapter.

In many countries, shellfish are embraced as food rather gingerly; in others they are wholeheartedly adopted. The perceived difficulty of preparing them may have something to do with it, but whether eaten raw, or marinated, stuffed, steamed, fried, boiled, baked or barbecued, shellfish offer flavours, aromas and textures that can be unbeatable. The recipes in this chapter have been chosen to show how shellfish can be used in dishes ranging from summer to winter, light to hearty, elaborate to surprisingly simple.

Like fish, shellfish need care when buying. Planning ahead is a necessary part of cooking with fish and shellfish, but it can also add to the pleasure. Once you have found a fishmonger you trust, you can be as adventurous as you like.

When buying shellfish, live specimens offer the best flavour, although many are available frozen. Crab and lobster are sometimes sold already cooked; the meat should smell sweet and look fresh. Cooked lobster tails should be tightly curled. Cephalopods are sold fresh and frozen, either fully intact or cleaned, and many larger fresh octopuses are also sold ready for use. If buying fresh cephalopods, use them within 1 to 2 days, or freeze fresh octopus for up to 3 months.

Live shellfish do not last long, so buy them on the day you intend to eat them and store in the refrigerator covered with a damp cloth. Always remove the dark intestinal tracts from prawns and lobsters and the stomach sacs from lobsters and crabs before cooking. Scrub any dirty shells and remove any barnacles. Drain and rinse once or twice more in water. The general rule for cooking shellfish is to do so either very briefly or for a very long time — anything in the middle tends to result in tough meat. In the following recipes, follow the preparation and cooking instructions carefully, and as with fish, if you buy good-quality shellfish from a reputable source, you have made the best of beginnings.

Vietnamese rice paper rolls

SERVES 4–6

Although this recipe may sound fiddly, once you've got the hang of making the rolls — which won't take long at all — you'll find this recipe super easy and quick. The rice paper rolls are very light and fresh tasting, and make a great light lunch or starter.

dried mung bean vermicelli	100 g (3½ oz)
rice paper wrappers	20–25, about 16 cm (6¼ inches) in diameter
mint	40 leaves
cooked prawns (shrimp)	20 large, cut in half horizontally
garlic chives	10, halved

dipping sauce

satay sauce	2 tablespoons
hoisin sauce	60 ml (2 fl oz/¼ cup)
red chilli	1, finely chopped
unsalted peanuts	1 tablespoon, chopped and roasted
lemon juice	1 tablespoon

Soak the vermicelli for 5 minutes in enough hot water to cover. Drain well and use scissors to roughly chop the noodles into shorter lengths.

Using a pastry brush, brush both sides of the rice paper wrappers with water. Leave for 2 minutes, or until wrappers become soft and pliable. Stack the wrappers on top of each other, sprinkling each lightly with water to prevent them sticking together and drying out. Be careful, as wrappers tear easily when softened.

Put one softened wrapper on a work surface and spoon about 1 tablespoon of noodles along the bottom third of the wrapper, leaving enough space at the sides to fold the wrapper over. Top with two mint leaves, two prawn halves and half a garlic chive. Fold in the sides towards each other and firmly roll up the wrapper, allowing the garlic chive to point out of one side. Repeat with the remaining wrappers and ingredients and put the rolls, seam side down, on a serving plate.

To make the dipping sauce, combine the satay sauce, hoisin sauce, red chilli, peanuts and lemon juice in a small bowl and mix thoroughly. Serve with the rolls.

Brush both sides of each rice paper wrapper with water.

Put the vermicelli into a bowl and use scissors to cut them up.

Roll up the rice paper wrapper to firmly enclose the filling.

Crab bisque

SERVES 4

Bisque is a seasoned purée of shellfish flavoured with cream and brandy, which is used as the basis of a soup. The shells of the featured seafood — such as crab, crayfish or lobster — are traditionally used to add flavour and a small amount of the flesh is often reserved as a garnish.

live crabs	1 kg (2 lb 4 oz)
butter	50 g (1¾ oz)
carrot	½, finely chopped
onion	½, finely chopped
celery	1 stalk, finely chopped
bay leaf	1
thyme	2 sprigs
tomato paste (concentrated purée)	2 tablespoons
brandy	2 tablespoons
dry white wine	150 ml (5 fl oz)
fish stock	1 litre (35 fl oz/4 cups)
medium grain rice	60 g (2¼ oz/⅓ cup)
thick (double/heavy) cream	60 ml (2 fl oz/¼ cup)
cayenne pepper	¼ teaspoon, or to taste

Freeze the crabs for 1–2 hours to immobilize them, then drop them into boiling water and cook just until the shells turn red. Remove with tongs and set aside until cool enough to handle.

Detach the claws and legs. Reserve 4 of the claws to use as a garnish. Crack any remaining claws and the legs, removing any meat and reserving the meat and shells separately. Snap off the flap on the underside of the body, then turn over and pull the top shell away from the bottom shell. Remove and discard the feathery gills and stomach sac and snap off the mouth. Pick the meat out of the shells, reserving meat and shells separately.

Heat the butter in a large saucepan. Add the vegetables, bay leaf and thyme and cook over medium heat for 3 minutes, without allowing vegetables to colour. Add reserved crab shells, tomato paste, brandy and white wine and then simmer for 2 minutes, or until reduced by half.

Add the stock and 500 ml (17 fl oz/2 cups) water and bring to the boil. Reduce the heat and simmer for 5 minutes. Remove the shells and finely crush them in a mortar and pestle (or in a food processor with a little of the stock). Return the crushed shells to the soup with the rice and the reserved crab meat. Bring to the boil, reduce the heat, cover and simmer for about 20 minutes, or until the rice is soft.

Immediately strain the bisque into a clean saucepan through a fine sieve lined with damp muslin, pressing down firmly on the solids to extract all the liquid. Add the cream and season with salt and cayenne pepper, then gently reheat. Ladle into warmed soup bowls and garnish with the crab claws.

Shellfish substitution lobster, prawns

Bouillabaisse

This French stew was traditionally made in large cauldrons on the beach by fishermen. It contained the fish that was least suitable for market, such as rascasse (rockfish), as well as various shellfish. Use firm fish, such as sea bass, snapper or red mullet; lobster and crab are good, too.

rouille	
red capsicum (pepper)	1 small
white bread	1 slice, crusts removed
red chilli	1
garlic	2 cloves
egg yolk	1
olive oil	80 ml (2¹/₂ fl oz/¹/₃ cup)
oil	2 tablespoons
fennel bulb	1, thinly sliced
onion	1, chopped
vine-ripened tomatoes	750 g (1 lb 10 oz)
tomato paste (concentrated purée)	4 tablespoons
fish stock or water	1.25 litres (44 fl oz/5 cups)
saffron threads	a pinch
bouquet garni	1
orange zest	5 cm (2 inch) piece
fish fillets	1.5 kg (3 lb 5 oz), cut into bite-sized pieces
black mussels	18, cleaned (see page 173)
bread or toast	to serve

To make the rouille, preheat grill (broiler). Cut the capsicum in half lengthways, remove the seeds and membrane and place, skin side up, under the hot grill until the skin blackens and blisters. (Alternatively, hold the capsicum over the gas flame of your stove until the skin is blackened.) Allow to cool before peeling away the skin. Roughly chop the capsicum flesh. Soak the bread in 60 ml (2 fl oz/¹/₄ cup) water, then squeeze dry with your hands. Put the capsicum, bread, chilli, garlic and egg yolk in a mortar and pestle or food processor and pound or mix together. Gradually add the oil in a thin stream, pounding or mixing until the rouille is smooth and has the texture of thick mayonnaise. Cover and refrigerate until needed.

Heat the oil in a large saucepan and cook the fennel and onion for 5 minutes, or until golden.

Meanwhile, score a cross in the base of each tomato. Cover with boiling water for 30 seconds, then plunge into cold water. Drain and peel skin away from the cross. Chop the tomatoes, discarding the cores. Add the chopped tomato to the saucepan and cook for 3 minutes. Stir in the stock, saffron, bouquet garni and orange zest, bring to the boil and boil for 10 minutes.

Remove the bouquet garni and orange zest and either push the soup through a sieve or purée in a blender. Return the soup to the cleaned saucepan, season well and bring back to the boil. Reduce the heat to a simmer and add the fish and mussels. Cook for 5 minutes, or until the fish is tender and the mussels have opened. Throw away any mussels that haven't opened in this time. Serve the soup with the rouille and bread or toast.

Note A bouquet garni is used for flavouring soups and stews. You can buy dried ones in the supermarket (look near the rest of the herbs) or make your own by wrapping the green part of a leek around a bay leaf, a sprig of thyme, a sprig of parsley and celery leaves. Tie the bundle with kitchen string.

Roast or grill the capsicum until the skin blisters and blackens.

Using your hands, squeeze dry the soaked bread.

Lobster soup with zucchini and avocado   SERVES 4

To ensure quality, buy a live lobster or, if necessary, a dead cooked one (never buy a dead uncooked lobster). To humanely kill a lobster, freeze it for 1–2 hours to immobilize it, then plunge it into boiling water and cook just until the shell turns red. To remove the meat, see page 104.

butter	50 g (1¾ oz)
garlic	1 clove, crushed
French shallots	2, finely chopped
onion	1, chopped
zucchini (courgette)	1, diced
dry white wine	2½ tablespoons
fish stock	400 ml (14 fl oz)
cooked lobster meat	250 g (9 oz), chopped
thick (double/heavy) cream	250 ml (9 fl oz/1 cup)
avocado	1, diced
coriander (cilantro) leaves	1 tablespoon, chopped
parsley	1 tablespoon, chopped
lemon juice	to serve

Melt the butter in a large saucepan. Add the garlic, chopped shallots, onion and zucchini and cook over medium heat for 8–10 minutes, or until the vegetables are just soft.

Add the wine and bring to the boil, keeping it on the boil for 3 minutes. Pour in the stock and bring to the boil again. Reduce the heat to low, add the lobster and simmer for 1–2 minutes, until warmed through. Gently stir in the cream. Season with salt and freshly ground black pepper.

Ladle the soup into 4 bowls and stir a little of the avocado, coriander and parsley into each one. Squeeze a little lemon juice over the soup before serving.

Shellfish substitution crayfish, prawns (shrimp)

Zucchini (courgettes) are baby marrows. There are pale green, dark green and yellow varieties. Baby zucchini are perfect for fresh, raw and lightly cooked dishes, while their larger, older siblings are definitely the go for heartier, slow-cooked dishes. When shopping, look for firm, unblemished zucchini. Eat as soon as possible after purchase, as refrigeration makes the texture deteriorate. There is no need to peel them; in fact, most of the flavour is in the skin. Zucchini flowers are also edible. They are a fleeting delight of summer, available for only a few weeks each year, and are often served stuffed and fried.

Rock lobster and mango salad

SERVES 4

When buying live lobsters, look for specimens that are lively and feel heavy, and that have a hard shell and no missing limbs. The lobster's tail should be tucked under the body. Large lobsters are cheaper, but weight for weight, smaller animals are better value.

live rock lobster	1 x 800 g (1 lb 12 oz)
sugar snap peas	100 g (3½ oz), trimmed
mango	1 large, cut into small chunks
spring onions (scallions)	2, trimmed and sliced into small pieces on the diagonal
orange capsicum (pepper)	½, thinly sliced
Lebanese cucumber	½, peeled, seeded and sliced into long thin batons

dressing
limes	zest and juice of 2
Thai fish sauce	1 tablespoon
red chilli	1 small, seeded and finely chopped
olive oil	2 tablespoons
sesame oil	1 teaspoon
dark soy sauce	1 teaspoon
sugar	½ teaspoon

Immobilize the live rock lobster by placing it in the freezer for 1 hour. Bring a large saucepan of salted water to the boil. Drop the lobster into the water and bring back to the boil. Cook for 25 minutes, by which time the lobster will have turned red. Lift out of the pan and leave to cool. Once cold, remove the cooked meat from the shell: firstly, remove the head by twisting or cutting it off. Cut down the centre of the underside of the tail with a pair of kitchen scissors. Peel open the tail and carefully pull out the flesh in one piece. Cut into chunks and then place in a large bowl.

Bring a small saucepan of water to the boil, add the sugar snap peas and blanch for 2 minutes. Refresh under cold running water, pat dry and add to lobster flesh with the mango, spring onions, capsicum and cucumber.

Mix dressing ingredients together in a pitcher and pour over the lobster and mango. Toss everything together and serve.

Shellfish substitution marron, yabbies, lobster

Remove the head of the cooked lobster by twisting.

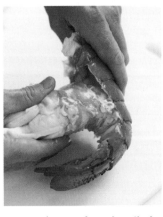
Remove the meat from the tail of the lobster in one piece.

Slice the tail meat crossways into large chunks.

Cuban-style prawns with rum

Always remove the black thread-like vein, or intestinal tract, from prawns (shrimp) before cooking them. With practice, this will come away along with the head of the prawn when it is pulled off. Or slit open the back of a peeled prawn with a small knife and remove the vein.

white rum	100 ml (3½ fl oz)
Tabasco sauce	a few drops
lime	zest and juice of 1
worcestershire sauce	2 teaspoons
plain (all-purpose) flour	2½ tablespoons
ground cumin	1 teaspoon
ground nutmeg	a generous pinch
raw tiger prawns (shrimp)	24, peeled and deveined, tails intact
butter	25 g (1 oz)
olive oil	80 ml (2½ fl oz/⅓ cup)
garlic	4 large cloves, crushed
flat-leaf (Italian) parsley	1 tablespoon, chopped
coriander (cilantro) leaves	1 tablespoon, chopped

In a small bowl, mix together the rum, Tabasco, lime zest and juice and worcestershire sauce.

Mix the flour with the cumin and nutmeg and season with salt and freshly ground black pepper. Dip the prawns in the seasoned flour to lightly coat before cooking.

Melt half the butter with half the oil in a large sauté or frying pan and when hot, add half the garlic and half the prawns. Cook for 4–5 minutes, or until the prawns have turned pink and are lightly golden on the outside. Lift onto a serving plate and keep warm. Repeat with the remaining butter, oil, garlic and prawns.

Pour the rum mixture into the pan and allow to bubble for 30–40 seconds, stirring. Season with salt. Mix together the parsley and coriander. Pour the sauce over the prawns and scatter with the herbs before serving.

Shellfish substitution freshwater crayfish

Prawns (shrimp) are found worldwide in cold and warm waters, but the lovely big tiger prawns (right) that are so welcome on summer barbecues are warm-water tropical creatures. In Australia, most tiger prawns are trawled, then put in ice-cold seawater to get them to market as fresh as possible. Elsewhere, huge farms have been established, leading to, in some cases, high incidence of disease and environmental problems. These concerns should not turn you off tiger prawns, rather encourage you to hunt out good-quality ones, as their taste, firm texture and versatility are worth it. Most supplies in the northern hemisphere are frozen; in this case, raw is better than cooked.

three ways with prawns

Unlike other crustaceans, prawns are not generally sold live. They may be sold raw or cooked, with or without their shells, or frozen. Whenever possible, buy them with the shell on, as they will have the best flavour. Prawns should look healthy and smell of the sea; any unpleasant or fishy smell usually means their flesh has started to deteriorate. Take care to cook prawns only until they turn pink and curl up; overcooking will make the flesh tough.

PRAWNS WITH GARLIC, CHILLI AND PARSLEY

Heat 25 g (1 oz) butter and 100 ml (3½ fl oz) olive oil together in a large frying pan. When hot, add 2 finely chopped large garlic cloves and 1 seeded and finely chopped small red chilli. Cook, stirring all the time, for 30 seconds. Add 24 large raw prawns (shrimp), peeled and deveined but with tails intact, and cook for 3–4 minutes on each side, or until they turn pink. Sprinkle prawns with 3 tablespoons chopped flat-leaf (Italian) parsley and serve immediately on hot plates, with lemon wedges. Serves 4.

DRUNKEN PRAWNS

Put 24 peeled and deveined large raw prawns (shrimp) in a non-metallic bowl. Mix 150 ml (5 fl oz) Chinese rice wine with 2 thinly sliced red chillies, 1 teaspoon finely grated fresh ginger and 2 teaspoons sugar and pour over prawns. Leave the mixture to marinate for 30 minutes. Heat a wok until very hot. Take 60 ml (2 fl oz/¼ cup) of the liquid out of the marinade and add to the wok. Heat it until it is very hot, then light it either with a match or by tipping the side of the wok towards the gas flame. Let the flame burn and die down before adding the rest of the marinade and prawns. Cook for 2–3 minutes, or until the prawns turn pink. Serve immediately. Serves 4.

Note Chinese rice wine (also called Shaoxing rice wine) is a fermented rice wine with a rich, sweetish taste, similar to dry sherry.

TANDOORI PRAWN PIZZA

Preheat oven to 220°C (425°F/Gas 7). To make the tandoori sauce, heat 1 tablespoon olive oil in a frying pan over medium heat. Add 2 teaspoons ground paprika, ½ teaspoon ground cumin, ¼ teaspoon ground cardamom, ¼ teaspoon ground ginger and ¼ teaspoon cayenne pepper. Cook until the oil starts to bubble, then cook for a further minute. Stir in 90 g (3¼ oz/⅓ cup) Greek-style yoghurt, 1 teaspoon lemon juice and 2 crushed garlic cloves, then add 16 large raw prawns (shrimp), peeled and deveined, tails intact. Cook for 5 minutes, or until prawns turn pink. Remove the prawns from the tandoori sauce with a slotted spoon and spread sauce over a 30 cm (12 inch) ready-made pizza base, leaving a 1 cm (½ inch) border. Slice 1 onion and 1 small red capsicum (pepper) and sprinkle half of each over the pizza base. Arrange the prawns on top. Top with the remaining onion and capsicum and bake for about 20 minutes. Scatter with 3 tablespoons torn basil, then serve with dollops of extra Greek-style yoghurt. Serves 4.

prawns with garlic, chilli and parsley

Warm prawn, rocket and feta salad

SERVES 6

Rocket (arugula) and prawns (shrimp) seem to have a particular affinity, with the peppery bite of the leaves complementing the sweet, firm flesh of the prawns. This salad is perfect for the height of summer, when ripe, juicy tomatoes are at their best and most abundant.

spring onions (scallions)	4, chopped
roma (plum) tomatoes	4, chopped
red capsicum (pepper)	1, chopped
canned chickpeas	400 g (14 oz), rinsed and drained
dill	1 tablespoon chopped
basil	3 tablespoons finely shredded
extra virgin olive oil	60 ml (2 fl oz/¼ cup)
butter	60 g (2¼ oz)
raw prawns (shrimp)	1 kg (2 lb 4 oz), peeled and deveined, tails intact
red chillies	2 small, finely chopped
garlic	4 cloves, crushed
lemon juice	2 tablespoons
wild or baby rocket (arugula)	300 g (10½ oz/2 bunches)
feta cheese	150 g (5½ oz)

Put the spring onion, tomato, capsicum, chickpeas, dill and shredded basil in a large bowl and toss together well.

Heat the oil and butter in a large frying pan or wok, add the prawns and cook, stirring, over high heat for 3 minutes. Add the chilli and garlic and continue cooking for 2 minutes, or until the prawns turn pink. Remove the pan from the heat and stir in the lemon juice.

Gently toss the rocket leaves with the tomato and chickpea mixture. Divide among 6 serving plates and top each with an equal amount of the prawn mixture. Crumble the feta cheese over the top and serve.

The chickpea is a small legume whose lineage goes back to Ancient Egypt and the Levant. It is still popular in those areas, as well as in parts of the Mediterranean, the Middle East and India. Dried chickpeas need long soaking and long cooking to render them soft; canned chickpeas need only thorough rinsing before use. Chickpeas have a meaty sweetness to them and famous uses include dishes such as hummus, felafel and Indian dhal. In combination with seafood, prawns (shrimp) seem to be the standout choice — the filling nature of chickpeas nicely balancing the lighter flavour of prawns and other summer salad ingredients.

Sugar cane prawns with dipping sauce   MAKES 8

It may be difficult to find fresh pieces of sugar cane. Cans of peeled, ready-to-use cane pieces are available from some Asian supermarkets. Or look for packaged pieces, which have been boiled to make them edible; peel away the brownish skin from the white flesh before using.

raw prawns (shrimp)	400 g (14 oz), peeled and deveined
egg white	1
ground coriander	1 teaspoon
red Asian shallots	2, peeled and roughly chopped
garlic	3 cloves, peeled and roughly chopped
palm sugar	1 teaspoon grated, or soft brown sugar
fish sauce	1 teaspoon
lemon grass	1 stem, white part only, cut into three pieces
Vietnamese mint or other mint leaves	1 tablespoon chopped
salt	1 teaspoon
sugar cane	8 x 10 cm (4 inch) thin lengths, about 1 cm (½ inch) in diameter, peeled (if the pieces are thick, cut them lengthways into quarters)
oil	for deep-frying

dipping sauce

rice vinegar	1 tablespoon
lime juice	1 tablespoon
fish sauce	1 tablespoon
sambal oelek	¼ teaspoon (see note)
sugar	1 teaspoon
cucumber	1 tablespoon, peeled and finely diced

Put prawns in a food processor with half the egg white, ground coriander, shallots, garlic, palm sugar, fish sauce, lemon grass, mint and salt. Process to a paste. Alternatively, chop finely and mix by hand. Add just enough of the remaining egg white to bind the mixture. Tip mixture out onto a large plate. Cover and chill for 30 minutes in the refrigerator.

Combine all ingredients for the dipping sauce in a small bowl.

Divide the prawn mixture into 8 equal portions. Put a portion of the prawn mixture in the palm of your hand. Press the end of a piece of sugar cane into the middle of the mixture, then firmly mould the mixture around the cane in a sausage shape so that it covers about 6 cm (2½ inches) of the cane. Transfer to a board and repeat with the remaining prawn mixture and pieces of cane to make 8 sugar cane prawns in total.

Fill a deep-fryer or large saucepan one-third full of oil. Heat the oil to 180°C (350°F), or until a cube of white bread dropped into the oil browns in 15 seconds.

Cook 3 or 4 prawn sticks at a time for 4–5 minutes, or until the prawn mixture turns a light golden brown. Turn halfway through cooking to ensure they brown evenly. Remove and drain on crumpled paper towels. Cool for a few minutes before serving with the dipping sauce.

Note Sambal oelek is a hot paste made from fresh red chillies and other seasonings. It is sold in some Asian supermarkets and will keep for months if stored in the refrigerator.

three ways with mayonnaise

Mayonnaise is simply an emulsion of egg yolks, salt, oil, and acid such as vinegar, and sometimes mustard or other flavourings. Making your own mayonnaise is well worth the effort. Have ingredients at room temperature, and when you start to mix, always add the oil drop by drop. Once mayonnaise has begun to emulsify, continue adding the oil in a slow stream. If it curdles, simply add the mixture, a little at a time, to another egg yolk, beating well after each addition.

LIME MAYONNAISE

Put 2 large egg yolks in a bowl along with a little salt and freshly ground black pepper and gently mix together with a whisk. Mix 150 ml (5 fl oz) each of peanut oil and olive oil together in a pitcher. Slowly add the oil to the egg yolks, drop by drop, whisking all the time. Increase to a slow trickle as the mayonnaise begins to thicken. Fold in the zest of 1 lime, the juice of half the lime and 1 tablespoon chopped dill. Taste the mayonnaise and season to your liking with a little extra lime juice, salt and freshly ground black pepper if needed. Serve with cold cooked seafood such as lobster, prawns (shrimp), and white fish. Serves 4.

HERB AÏOLI

Put 4 egg yolks, 4 crushed garlic cloves, 1 tablespoon chopped basil, 4 tablespoons chopped flat-leaf (Italian) parsley and 1 tablespoon lemon juice in a mortar or food processor. Pound with the pestle or process until light and creamy. Add 200 ml (7 fl oz) olive oil, drop by drop, from the tip of a teaspoon, pounding or processing constantly until the mixture begins to thicken. At this point, add the oil in a steady stream until all the oil is incorporated and the mayonnaise is thick. (If you are using a food processor, pour in the oil in a thin stream with the motor running.) This sauce goes well with a range of cooked seafood such as lobster, mussels, scallops, prawns (shrimp) and salmon. Serves 4.

VODKA AND CHILLI MAYONNAISE

Seed and finely chop 1–2 small red chillies and put in a mortar or food processor with 4 egg yolks. Pound with the pestle or process until the mixture is light and creamy and the chilli is well mixed in. Add 150 ml (5 fl oz) olive oil, drop by drop, from the tip of a teaspoon, pounding or processing constantly until the mixture begins to thicken. At this point, add the oil in a steady stream until all the oil is incorporated and the mayonnaise is thick. (If you are using a food processor, pour in the oil in a thin stream with the motor running.) Add 2 teaspoons vodka, season with salt and freshly ground black pepper and mix well. Makes 200 ml (7 fl oz). Serves 4.

Note This sauce goes well with smoked salmon or trout, or most types of cold cooked seafood.

prawns with lime mayonnaise

Mexican seafood stew with avocado salsa   SERVES 4

After being introduced to Mexico by the invading Spaniards more than 400 years ago, coriander (cilantro) was quickly embraced in local dishes, as its strong, fresh flavour complements the spiciness of their ever-popular chilli.

olive oil	60 ml (2 fl oz/¼ cup)
onion	1 large, chopped
celery	1 large stalk, about 100 g (3½ oz), chopped
garlic	3 cloves, crushed
thin red chillies	2 small, seeded and finely chopped
fish stock	200 ml (7 fl oz)
canned roma (plum) tomatoes	800 g (1 lb 12 oz)
bay leaves	2
dried oregano	1 teaspoon
caster (superfine) sugar	1 teaspoon
corn	2 large cobs, kernels removed
halibut fillets	500 g (1 lb 2 oz), skinned
coriander (cilantro) leaves	2 tablespoons chopped
limes	juice of 2
raw tiger prawns (shrimp)	12, peeled and deveined, tails intact
scallops	8
clams	12, cleaned
thick (double/heavy) cream	125 ml (4 fl oz/½ cup)

avocado salsa

avocado	½ small
red onion	½ small, finely chopped
coriander (cilantro) leaves	1 tablespoon chopped
lime	finely grated zest and juice of 1

Heat the oil in a large saucepan. Add the onion and celery and cook over a medium–low heat for 10 minutes, stirring now and then. Add the garlic and chillies and cook for 1 minute, stirring. Add the fish stock and tomatoes and break the tomatoes up in the pan using a wooden spoon.

Stir in bay leaves, oregano and sugar and bring to the boil. Allow to bubble for 2 minutes, then reduce heat to low and gently simmer for 10 minutes. Allow to cool for 5 minutes, then remove the bay leaves and tip the mixture into a food processor or blender and whizz until fairly smooth, but still retaining some texture. Alternatively, push the mixture through a coarse sieve or mouli by hand.

Return the mixture to the pan and season with salt. Add the corn kernels and bring back to the boil. Reduce the heat to a simmer to cook for 3 minutes, or until the kernels are just tender. Cut the fish into large chunks.

Stir the coriander and lime juice into the mixture, add the fish, then simmer gently for 1 minute. Add the prawns and scallops and scatter clams on the top. Cover with a lid and then cook gently for a further 2–3 minutes, or until seafood is opaque and cooked through and clams have steamed open. Discard any clams that do not open during cooking.

While seafood is cooking, make the avocado salsa. Chop the avocado into small cubes and mix with red onion, coriander and lime zest and juice. Season with salt and freshly ground black pepper. Before serving, stir cream into the stew, ladle into deep bowls and serve with the salsa.

Fish substitution kingfish, snapper

Using a sieve or mouli, purée the tomato mixture.

Add the seafood to the pan and steam until the clams open.

Herbed bugs with sweet cider sauce

SERVES 4

The curiously-named bugs are flat crustaceans that have a somewhat prehistoric appearance and a flesh similar to that of crayfish. They need only brief cooking.

bugs	16
olive oil	80 ml (2½ fl oz/⅓ cup)
lemon juice	150 ml (5 fl oz)
garlic	3 cloves, crushed
flat-leaf (Italian) parsley	a large handful finely chopped
dill	3 tablespoons finely chopped, plus extra, to garnish
apple cider	80 ml (2½ fl oz/⅓ cup)
butter	40 g (1½ oz)
crusty bread and green salad	to serve

Remove the heads from the bugs, then cut them in half lengthways. Put in a single layer in a shallow non-metallic dish. Combine the olive oil, lemon juice, garlic, parsley and dill, and pour over the bugs. Cover and refrigerate for at least 1 hour.

Preheat a chargrill pan or barbecue flatplate to high. Cook the bugs, shell side down, for 2 minutes. Turn and cook for another 2 minutes, or until tender. Transfer to a serving platter.

Simmer the apple cider in a small saucepan until reduced by two-thirds. Reduce the heat and add the butter, stirring until melted. Remove from the heat, pour over the bugs and serve. Serve with crusty bread and a green salad.

Shellfish substitution scampi, crayfish

Bugs (also known as flathead, slipper or shovel-nosed lobsters, or balmain or moreton bay bugs) belong to the family Scyllaridae, and are found all over the world. Thier name translates to 'sea cricket' in French, Italian and Spanish, due to the cricket-like snapping noise that they make in the water, and which is audible to fishermen. All species have the same general shape and characteristics, but vary in size and colour from the 45 cm (18inch) Mediterranean types to Indo-Pacific species of up to 25 cm (10 inches). They are less well known than true lobsters, but their meat — which is contained in the tail section — can be prepared in a similar way.

three ways with crab

To ensure freshness, buy live crabs and cook them yourself. First, freeze the crab for 1 hour to immobilize it, then plunge into boiling water for 10–15 minutes per 500 g (1 lb 2 oz). The shells will change to orange-red when cooked. With a large knife or cleaver, cut the crabs into quarters. Pull the intestines and grey gills out of the bodies and crack the claws using crab crackers or the back of a heavy knife. Remove the crab meat from the claws and bodies.

CRAB CAKES WITH AVOCADO SALSA

Put 350 g (12 oz) fresh crab meat in a bowl. Pick out any stray pieces of shell or cartilage. Add 2 lightly beaten eggs, 1 finely chopped spring onion (scallion), 1 tablespoon mayonnaise, 2 teaspoons sweet chilli sauce and 100 g (3½ oz/1¼ cups) fresh white breadcrumbs. Season with salt and freshly ground black pepper, then stir well. Using wet hands, form crab mixture into 8 flat patties. Cover and refrigerate for 30 minutes. Meanwhile, make the avocado salsa. Put 2 chopped vine-ripened roma (plum) tomatoes, 1 finely chopped small red onion, 1 diced large ripe avocado, 60 ml (2 fl oz/¼ cup) lime juice, 2 tablespoons chervil leaves and ½ teaspoon caster (superfine) sugar in a bowl. Season to taste with salt and freshly ground black pepper, then toss gently. Heat 60 ml (2 fl oz/¼ cup) oil in a large frying pan over medium heat. Dust patties with plain (all-purpose) flour and shallow-fry them for 3 minutes on each side, or until golden brown — only turn once so they don't break up. Drain on crumpled paper towels. Serve crab cakes with the avocado salsa (or use the tomato salsa on page 127) and lime wedges, if desired. Serves 4.

Shellfish substitution tinned or thawed frozen crab meat

CHAR KWAY TEOW WITH CRAB

Put 150 g (5½ oz) dried thin rice noodles in a bowl and cover with boiling water. Leave to soak for 10 minutes, then drain. Heat 60 ml (2 fl oz/¼ cup) oil in a wok and when hot, add 2 thinly sliced shallots, 1 finely chopped garlic clove and 2 finely chopped small chillies. Cook for 5 minutes, stirring. Add 175 g (6 oz) bean sprouts and 175 g (6 oz) finely chopped Chinese barbecued pork and cook for 2 minutes. Add 60 ml (2 fl oz/¼ cup) light soy sauce, 2 tablespoons oyster sauce, noodles, 500 g (1 lb 2 oz) fresh crab meat and 2 tablespoons chopped coriander (cilantro) leaves. Stir over heat for 2 minutes to heat through. Season with salt. Serves 4.

Note You will need 6 live crabs, each weighing about 250 g (9 oz), to get this amount of crab meat.

Shellfish substitution tinned or thawed frozen crab meat

SPAGHETTI WITH CRAB AND AVOCADO

Cook 350 g (12 oz) spaghetti according to the packet instructions. Drain and set aside. Meanwhile, put 200 g (7 oz) fresh crab meat in a bowl and pick out any stray pieces of shell or cartilage. Separate the meat into individual pieces. Peel a large avocado and cut into small cubes. Add to the crab along with a handful of flat-leaf (Italian) parsley leaves. In a small bowl, combine 100 ml (3½ fl oz) olive oil and 2 tablespoons lemon juice and season well with salt and freshly ground black pepper. Pour over the crab mixture and gently toss to mix. Add the pasta and toss again gently. Serve immediately on warm plates. Serves 4 as a starter.

Shellfish substitution tinned or thawed frozen crab meat

crab cakes with avocado salsa

Har gow

Har gow are one of the many dim sum so enjoyed by the Chinese at breakfast or lunch. These snack-like morsels come in steamed, fried and deep-fried varieties, and have been part of Cantonese cuisine since the Sung Dynasty nearly 1,000 years ago.

filling

prawns (shrimp)	500 g (1 lb 2 oz), peeled and deveined
pork or bacon fat	50 g (1¾ oz), rind removed and finely diced
bamboo shoots	40 g (1½ oz) finely chopped
spring onion (scallion)	1, finely chopped
sugar	1 teaspoon
soy sauce	3 teaspoons
roasted sesame oil	½ teaspoon
egg white	1, lightly beaten
salt	1 teaspoon
cornflour (cornstarch)	1 tablespoon

dough

wheat starch	175 g (6 oz)
cornflour (cornstarch)	3 teaspoons
oil	2 teaspoons
soy sauce or hot chilli sauce	to serve

To make filling, cut half of the prawns into 1 cm (½ inch) chunks. Chop the remaining prawns using a knife or food processor until finely minced (ground). Combine all prawns in a large bowl. Add the pork or bacon fat, bamboo shoots, spring onion, sugar, soy sauce, sesame oil, egg white, salt and cornflour. Mix well to combine.

To make dough, put wheat starch, cornflour and oil in a small bowl. Add 250 ml (9 fl oz/1 cup) boiling water and mix until well combined. Add a little extra flour if dough is too sticky.

Roll the dough into a long cylinder and divide into 24 pieces. Cover pieces with a damp tea towel. Using a rolling pin and working with one portion of dough at a time, roll out to a 9–10 cm (3½–4 inch) round (you may find this easier if you put the dough between two pieces of oiled plastic wrap).

Put 1 teaspoon of the filling in the centre of each wrapper and fold the wrapper over to make a half-moon shape. Spread a little water along the edge of the wrapper and use your thumb and index finger to form small pleats along the outside edge. With the other hand, press the two opposite edges together to seal. The inside edge should curve in a semicircle to conform to the shape of the pleated edge. Put the har gow in 2 bamboo steamers lined with greaseproof paper punched with holes. Cover the har gow as you work to prevent them drying out. If you do not have 2 bamboo steamers, cook har gow in 2 batches.

Cover and steam the har gow over simmering water in a wok, swapping steamers halfway through, for 6–8 minutes, or until wrappers are translucent. Serve with soy or hot chilli sauce.

Roll out portions of dough, one at a time, into rounds.

Fold the dough over the filling then pleat the edges.

Cajun devilled crab

The term 'devilled' denotes a dish that is coated or topped with breadcrumbs and served with a spicy sauce. If using fresh crabs for this recipe, reserve shells and serve the devilled crab in them; the mixture makes enough to fill 4 small to medium shells.

butter	25 g (1 oz)
plain (all-purpose) flour	1½ tablespoons
milk	225 ml (7½ fl oz)
thick (double/heavy) cream	60 ml (2 fl oz/¼ cup)
dijon mustard	1 tablespoon
worcestershire sauce	1 teaspoon
cayenne pepper	a pinch
paprika	a pinch
lemon juice	2 teaspoons
flat-leaf (Italian) parsley	2 tablespoons finely chopped
cooked crab meat	100 g (3½ oz)
Tabasco sauce	1 or 2 drops
white bread	25 g (1 oz)
parmesan cheese	25 g (1 oz) grated

Melt the butter in a saucepan. Add the flour and combine to make a roux. Remove the pan from the heat and gradually add the milk, stirring after each addition. Return to the heat and gently bring back to the boil, stirring constantly until thick.

Take the saucepan off the heat again and stir in the cream, mustard, worcestershire sauce, cayenne pepper, paprika, lemon juice, half the parsley and the crab meat. Add the Tabasco sauce and season with salt.

Preheat the oven to 200°C (400°F/Gas 6). Put the bread in a food processor and process to fine breadcrumbs or grate it on a coarse grater. Mix with the cheese and the remaining parsley.

Spoon the crab mixture into the empty crab shells or use dishes with a 150 ml (5 fl oz) capacity and sprinkle the breadcrumb mixture over the top. Put on a baking tray and heat in the oven for 10 minutes, or until the mixture is bubbling and the breadcrumbs are golden brown.

It is best to buy crabs that are alive – choose lively ones that feel heavy for their size. Never buy dead uncooked crabs. If buying cooked crabs, they should smell fresh and be undamaged, with their limbs drawn into the body. To humanely kill a crab, put it in the freezer for at least 45 minutes, then drop it into a saucepan of boiling, salted water. Simmer for 15 minutes per 500 g (1 lb 2 oz). To remove the meat from a cooked crab, snap off the flap on the underside, then turn over and pull the top shell away from the bottom shell. Remove the feathery gills and stomach sac and snap off the mouth. Pick the meat out of the shells, keeping dark and white meat separate. Twist off and crack the legs and claws and take out any meat.

three ways with barbecued shellfish

To prepare and clean squid or octopus, cut or gently pull the tentacles away from the tube; the intestines should come away with them. Cut under the eyes to remove intestines from the tentacles, then remove the beak (if it remains in the centre of the tentacles) by using your fingers to push up the centre. Pull away the soft bone. Rub the tubes under cold running water and the skin should come away easily. Wash the tubes and tentacles and drain well.

BARBECUED SQUID WITH GARLIC AND PARSLEY DRESSING

First, prepare and clean 750 g (1 lb 10 oz) small squid (see above), or ask your fishmonger to do it for you. Put the tubes and tentacles in a bowl, add 1/4 teaspoon salt and mix well. Cover and refrigerate for about 30 minutes. Heat a barbecue flatplate. Meanwhile, make the picada dressing. Whisk together 60 ml (2 fl oz/1/4 cup) extra virgin olive oil, 3 tablespoons finely chopped flat-leaf (Italian) parsley, 2 crushed garlic cloves, 1/2 teaspoon freshly ground black pepper and some salt in a small pitcher or bowl. When ready to cook the squid, lightly oil the barbecue flatplate and cook the squid in small batches for 2–3 minutes, or until the tubes are white and tender. Barbecue the squid tentacles for 1 minute, or until they curl up and are brown all over. Serve hot, drizzled with the dressing, and accompanied by rocket (arugula) leaves and crusty bread. Serves 4.

Shellfish substitution cuttlefish, octopus, prawns (shrimp) or chunks of firm white fish fillet

BARBECUED ASIAN-STYLE SEAFOOD

Peel and devein 500 g (1 lb 2 oz) raw prawns (shrimp), leaving the tails intact. Prepare and clean 500 g (1 lb 2 oz) baby squid and cut the tubes into quarters. Clean 500 g (1 lb 2 oz) baby octopus. (Or ask your fishmonger to clean both for you.) Put the seafood into a shallow non-metallic bowl along with 300 g (10 1/2 oz) scallop meat. In a separate bowl, combine 250 ml (9 fl oz/1 cup) sweet chilli sauce, 1 tablespoon fish sauce, 2 tablespoons lime juice and 1 tablespoon peanut oil. Pour mixture over the seafood and mix gently to coat. Allow to marinate in the refrigerator for 1 hour. Drain the seafood and reserve the marinade. Heat 2 tablespoons peanut oil on a barbecue flatplate or chargrill pan. Cook seafood, in batches if necessary, over high heat for 3–5 minutes, or until tender. Drizzle each batch with a little of the leftover marinade during cooking. Serve with steamed rice with lime wedges. Serves 6.

HONEY AND LIME PRAWN KEBABS WITH TOMATO SALSA

Peel and devein 32 raw prawns (shrimp), leaving the tails intact. Put them in a non-metallic dish. Whisk together 90 g (3 1/4 oz/1/4 cup) honey, 1 seeded and finely chopped small red chilli, 2 tablespoons olive oil, the zest and juice of 2 limes, 1 crushed large garlic clove, a 2 cm (3/4 inch) piece of fresh ginger, finely grated, and 1 tablespoon chopped coriander (cilantro) leaves. Pour marinade over prawns, toss well, cover and refrigerate for at least 3 hours, turning occasionally. Soak 8 bamboo skewers in water for 30 minutes. Meanwhile, make the salsa. Score a cross in the base of 2 tomatoes. Cover with boiling water for 30 seconds, then plunge into cold water. Peel the skin away from the cross. Dice the tomatoes, discarding the cores and saving any juice. In a bowl, mix the tomato flesh and juice with 1 diced small just-ripe mango, 1/2 diced small red onion, 1 seeded and finely chopped small red chilli, the zest and juice of 1 lime and 2 tablespoons chopped coriander leaves. Preheat griller (broiler) or a barbecue flatplate to high. Thread 4 prawns onto each skewer. Cook for 4 minutes, turning halfway through cooking and basting regularly with leftover marinade, until the prawns turn pink and are lightly browned on both sides. Serve the kebabs with salsa and steamed rice. Serves 4.

barbecued squid with garlic and parsley dressing

Zarzuela

This Catalan fish soup is named after a style of light opera, which gives some idea of its vitality. It incorporates a variety of seafood, and is built around a picada. This blend of garlic, nuts and bread acts like a roux to give form to, or hold together, dishes.

sofrito base

tomatoes	2 large, peeled
olive oil	1 tablespoon
onions	2, finely chopped
tomato paste (concentrated purée)	1 tablespoon

picada

white bread	3 slices, crusts removed
almonds	1 tablespoon, roasted
garlic	3 cloves
olive oil	1 tablespoon

lobster tail	1 raw, about 400 g (14 oz)
firm white fish fillets such as cod, warehou or flake	750 g (1 lb 10 oz), skinned and cut into bite-sized pieces
plain (all-purpose) flour	for coating
olive oil	2–3 tablespoons
squid tubes	125 g (4½ oz), cleaned and cut into rings
raw large prawns (shrimp)	12
dry white wine	125 ml (4 fl oz/½ cup)
black mussels	12–15, cleaned
brandy	125 ml (4 fl oz/½ cup)
flat-leaf (Italian) parsley	3 tablespoons, chopped

Score a cross in the base of the tomatoes. Place in a heatproof bowl and cover with boiling water. Leave for 30 seconds then transfer to cold water and peel the skin away from the cross. To seed, cut each tomato in half and scoop out the seeds with a teaspoon. Chop the tomato flesh.

To make sofrito, heat the oil in a large flameproof casserole dish on the stovetop. Add the onion and stir for 5 minutes without browning. Add chopped tomato, tomato paste and 125 ml (4 fl oz/½ cup) water and stir for 10 minutes. Stir in another 125 ml (4 fl oz/½ cup) water, season and set aside.

To make the picada, finely chop bread, almonds and garlic in a food processor or by hand. With the motor running, or continuously stirring, gradually add the oil to form a paste.

Preheat the oven to 180°C (350°F/Gas 4). Cut the lobster tail into rounds through the membrane that separates the shell segments and set aside. Season the flour with salt and freshly ground black pepper and use it to coat the fish pieces. Heat the oil in a large frying pan and fry fish pieces in batches over medium heat for 2–3 minutes, or until cooked and golden brown all over. Add to the casserole dish with the sofrito.

Add a little oil to the frying pan if necessary, add the squid and cook, stirring, for 1–2 minutes. Remove and then add it to the casserole. Cook lobster and prawns for 2–3 minutes, or until just pink, then add to casserole. Add the wine to the frying pan and bring to the boil. Reduce the heat, add the mussels, cover and steam for 4–5 minutes. Add to the casserole, discarding any unopened mussels.

Pour brandy into the same pan, ignite and when the flames have died down, pour over the seafood. Mix well, cover and bake for 20 minutes. Stir in picada and cook for 10 minutes more, or until warmed through — do not overcook, or the seafood will toughen. Sprinkle with the parsley.

Note Raw lobster tails are available frozen.

Crayfish with dill and melted butter

SERVES 2

Crayfish are small freshwater crustaceans, similar in appearance and habits to lobster. There are many types, some of the best known being ecrevisse in France, crawfish in the United States, and yabbies and marrons in Australia. Choose crayfish that feel heavy for their size.

live freshwater crayfish	450 g (1 lb)
salt	1 tablespoon
sugar	2 tablespoons
dill	4 large sprigs
lemons	2
butter	100 g (3½ oz)

Immobilize the crayfish by putting them in the freezer 1 hour before you plan to cook them.

Bring a large saucepan of water to the boil with the salt, sugar, 2 dill sprigs and 1 lemon, cut in half. Reduce heat to medium, add crayfish and simmer for 4–6 minutes depending on their size. The crayfish will float when they are cooked.

Meanwhile, melt the butter and season with salt and freshly ground black pepper. Chop remaining two sprigs of dill and stir into the butter.

Drain the crayfish well; to drain the claws thoroughly, make a small hole in each one to let any water out. To cut the crayfish in half, hold the tail firmly in one hand with a tea towel, plunge a large, sharp kitchen knife into the midpoint, where the tail meets the head, and slice quickly down. Next, slice lengthways through the tail. Discard the head.

Serve the crayfish tail and claws in a large bowl alongside the melted butter for dipping and the second lemon, cut into wedges. Provide finger bowls and napkins for cleaning up.

Shellfish substitution small lobster, langoustine, marrons and yabbies

Plunge the immobilized crayfish into the boiling cooking liquid.

Cut the cooked crayfish in half where the head and tail meet.

Slice the tail section in half lengthways.

the perfect tempura

Tempura is one of Japan's most widely recognized dishes. It is actually of Portuguese origin, and consists of bite-sized pieces of seafood or vegetables that are coated in a light batter and then deep-fried until crisp and puffed. The batter is usually nothing more than flour and water, although egg is sometimes added. The consistency and temperature of batter are the all-important factors in achieving beautifully crisp tempura. Both the batter and food must be kept cold until just before cooking, and to achieve light, crisp batter the cooking oil must be kept at a steady 180°C (350°F) throughout the cooking process (this is done by using a special thermometer). Tempura is usually served with a soy sauce-based dipping sauce. Tempura flour is an especially fine flour available from Japanese food stores and large supermarkets.

Prepare the seafood to be cooked by cutting each piece into bite-sized chunks. To serve 4 as an appetizer, or as a main meal with rice, use 200 g (7 oz) skinned fish fillets and 12 large prawns (shrimp). Skinned haddock fillets, bream, cod and rock cod are all good choices, as are squid, lobster and crayfish. Prawns are also delicious cooked this way; peel and devein prawns, leaving the tails intact, and make three cuts on underside of each prawn to straighten them out. Keep seafood in the refrigerator until ready to use it. To make enough batter for 4 servings, put 100 g (3½ oz) tempura flour in a bowl and use chopsticks to incorporate 160 ml (5¼ fl oz) ice-cold water. Mix until just combined but still lumpy — it is important not to beat lumps out. Add a few ice cubes to keep it cold.

Fill a deep-fryer or large saucepan one-third full of vegetable oil and heat to 180°C (350°F), or until a cube of white bread dropped into the oil browns in 15 seconds. Dip the fish chunks and prawns in the batter, allowing excess batter to drip off. Fry until crisp and golden. Drain on crumpled paper towels and serve immediately with a dipping sauce. Do not let the tempura sit around and do not reheat it, as it will become soggy.

To make your own dipping sauce, stir 1 teaspoon finely grated fresh ginger and ½ tablespoon mirin into 60 ml (2 fl oz/¼ cup) soy sauce. Dilute it to taste with up to 1½ tablespoons water. Pour the sauce into dipping bowls. This makes enough to serve 4.

Prawn pot pies

SERVES 4

Raw prawns (shrimp) should smell pleasantly of the sea. Reject any that smell off or fishy, or that have black heads or oozing black juices. Fresh raw prawns are the best choice, but frozen raw prawns may be used. Thaw them on a plate in the refrigerator, and cook without delay.

butter	60 g (2¼ oz)
leek	1, white part only, thinly sliced
garlic	1 clove, finely chopped
raw prawns (shrimp)	1 kg (2 lb 4 oz), peeled and deveined, tails intact
plain (all-purpose) flour	1 tablespoon
chicken or fish stock	185 ml (6 fl oz/¾ cup)
dry white wine	125 ml (4 fl oz/½ cup)
cream	500 ml (17 fl oz/2 cups)
lemon juice	2 tablespoons
dill	1 tablespoon chopped
flat-leaf (Italian) parsley	1 tablespoon chopped
dijon mustard	1 teaspoon
frozen puff pastry	1 sheet, just thawed
egg	1, lightly beaten
salad and bread	to serve (optional)

Preheat the oven to 220°C (425°F/Gas 7). Melt the butter in a saucepan over low heat. Cook the leek and garlic for 2 minutes, then add the prawns and cook for 1–2 minutes, or until just pink. Remove the prawns with a slotted spoon and set aside.

Stir the flour into the pan and cook for 1 minute. Add stock and wine, bring to the boil and cook for 10 minutes, or until most of the liquid has evaporated. Stir in cream, bring to the boil, then reduce the heat and simmer for 20 minutes, or until the liquid reduces by half. Stir in the lemon juice, herbs and mustard.

Using half of the sauce, pour an even amount into each of four 250 ml (9 fl oz/1 cup) ramekins. Divide the prawns among the ramekins, then top with the remaining sauce.

Cut the pastry into four rounds, slightly larger than the rim of the ramekins. Put the pastry rounds over the prawn mixture and press around the edges. Prick the pastry with a fork and brush with beaten egg. Bake for 20 minutes, or until the pastry is crisp and golden. Serve with a salad and bread, if desired.

Thinly slice the white part of the leek.

Cook the leek and garlic in the melted butter for 2 minutes.

Add the stock and wine to the butter and leek mixture.

Creamy clam soup

SERVES 4

Bivalve molluscs such as clams must always be alive when cooked. To check this, tip the shells into a sink filled with cold water and sort through them — they should all be closed. If any shells are open, tap them on the sink. If they stay open, throw them away, as they are dead.

clams	1.75 kg (4 lb), cleaned (see note)
fish stock	800 ml–1 litre (28–35 fl oz)
butter	50 g (1¾ oz)
onion	1, chopped
celery	1 stalk, chopped
carrot	1 large, chopped
leek	1 large, sliced into rings
swede (rutabaga)	250 g (9 oz), diced
bay leaf	1
medium- or short-grain rice	70 g (2½ oz/heaped ⅓ cup)
cream	200 ml (7 fl oz)
flat-leaf (Italian) parsley	3 tablespoons finely chopped

Put the clams and 250 ml (9 fl oz/1 cup) water in a large saucepan. Bring to the boil, then reduce the heat to medium and cover with a tight-fitting lid. Cook for 3–4 minutes, or until the shells open. Strain into a bowl. Add enough fish stock to make up to 1 litre (35 fl oz/4 cups). Discard any clams that haven't opened. Remove all but 8 of the clams from their shells.

Melt butter in a clean saucepan. Add vegetables and cook, covered, over medium heat for 10 minutes, stirring now and then. Add stock mixture and bay leaf, bring to the boil, then reduce heat and simmer for 10 minutes. Add rice, return to the boil, cover and cook over medium heat for 15 minutes, or until rice and vegetables are tender. Remove from heat and stir in clam meat. Remove bay leaf. Allow to cool for 10 minutes.

Purée soup until smooth, then return to a clean saucepan. Stir in the cream, season and gently reheat. Divide among 4 bowls, and add the parsley and two reserved clams to each bowl.

Shellfish substitution pipis

Note Even if you have bought clams, mussels, pipis or other bivalves as cleaned, put them in a bucket of seawater or heavily salted water for a couple of hours to ensure they expel all their grit. Then rinse under cold running water and drain well.

Cook the clams in the water until they open.

Remove the clam meat from the shells and set aside.

Japanese prawn, scallop and noodle soup   SERVES 4

Fresh scallops are superior to frozen ones, and avoid suspiciously plump, pure white specimens; they may have been soaked in water to bulk them up. Scallops, unlike most other bivalves, do not need to be soaked to purge them; just rinse them quickly under water to remove any sand.

dried shiitake mushrooms	4
dried soba or somen noodles	100 g (3½ oz)
bonito-flavoured soup stock	10 g (¼ oz) sachet
carrot	75 g (2½ oz), cut into thin batons
firm tofu	150 g (5½ oz), cut into cubes
raw prawns (shrimp)	16, peeled and deveined, tails intact
scallops	8, cleaned
spring onions (scallions)	2, finely chopped
mirin	1 tablespoon
shichimi togarashi	to serve (see note)

Soak the mushrooms in 300 ml (10½ fl oz) boiling water for 30 minutes. Meanwhile, cook noodles in a saucepan of boiling water for 2 minutes, or until just tender, then drain and rinse with cold water. Return the noodles to the pan and cover.

In a large saucepan, mix the stock with 1 litre (35 fl oz/4 cups) water. Drain mushrooms and add the soaking liquid to pan. Chop mushroom caps, discarding stalks. Add the mushrooms and carrot to the pan and bring the liquid to the boil. Reduce the heat to a simmer and cook for 5 minutes. Add tofu, prawns, scallops, spring onion and mirin to the pan. Cook at a gentle simmer for 4 minutes, or until prawns have turned pink and are cooked and the scallops are firm and opaque.

Meanwhile, pour hot water over the noodles and swish them around to separate and warm them. Drain. Divide the noodles among 4 large bowls and pour the soup over them, dividing the seafood equally. Serve, offering the shichimi togarashi as a flavouring to sprinkle on top.

Fish substitution chunks of firm white fish, fish balls

Note Shichimi togarashi is a Japanese condiment available from Japanese speciality stores.

Chop the caps of the soaked mushrooms, discarding the stalk.s

Cook the noodles in boiling water until just tender.

Simmer gently until the prawns are pink and the scallops opaque.

three ways with batter

The secret to successful deep-frying is to have the oil at the right temperature. A deep-frying thermometer is helpful here, or you can simply gauge the heat of the oil by putting a cube of white bread into the oil and seeing how long it takes to brown. At 160°C (315°F), it will brown in 30 seconds; at 180°C (350°F), it will take 15 seconds; and at 190°C (375°F), 10 seconds. For safety's sake, always lower foods gently into the oil rather than dropping them in.

BEER-BATTERED FISH WITH CRUNCHY CHIPS

Cut 8 floury potatoes such as desiree, pontiac or bintje into long 1 cm (½ inch) wide chips (fries), then soak them in cold water for 10 minutes. Drain and pat dry. Fill a deep-fryer or large saucepan one-third full of oil and heat to 160°C (315°F). Fry chips, in batches, for 4–5 minutes, or until lightly golden. Remove with a slotted spoon and drain on crumpled paper towels. Pat dry 4 skinned firm white fish fillets such as cod, haddock, snapper or perch, cut into strips and dust with cornflour (cornstarch). Maket batter at the last minute, as the bubbles in the beer help to make a better batter. To make batter, sift 80 g (2¾ oz) plain (all-purpose) flour into a large bowl and make a well in the centre. Gradually pour in 200 ml (7 fl oz) beer, whisking to make a smooth batter. Dip the fillets into the batter and shake off any excess. Gently lower the fillets into the oil and deep-fry in batches for 5–7 minutes, or until golden and cooked through. Turn with tongs if necessary. When cooked, the flesh should be moist and opaque. Drain on crumpled paper towels. Keep warm in a low oven while you cook the chips a second time. Reheat the oil to 180°C (350°F). Cook the chips for 1–2 minutes, again in batches, until crisp and golden. Drain on crumpled paper towels. Serve the fish with the chips and lemon wedges. Serves 4.

FRITTO MISTO DI MARE

To make batter, sift 210 g (7¼ oz/1⅔ cups) plain (all-purpose) flour and ¼ teaspoon salt into a bowl. Mix in 80 ml (2½ fl oz/⅓ cup) olive oil with a wooden spoon, then gradually add 300 ml (10½ fl oz/1¼ cups) tepid water, changing to a whisk when the mixture becomes liquid. Whisk until the batter is smooth and thick. Cover and leave to stand for 20 minutes in the refrigerator. Whisk 1 large egg white until stiff peaks form, then fold into batter. This batter goes well with a range of seafood: 250 g (9 oz) cleaned baby squid, 12 large prawns (shrimp), peeled and deveined, tails intact, 8 cleaned small octopus, 16 cleaned scallops, 12 fresh sardines, gutted and heads removed, and 250 g (9 oz) skinned fish fillets, cut into large cubes. To use, fill a deep-fryer or a large saucepan one-third full of oil and heat to 190°C (375°F). Dry seafood on paper towels. Working with one type of seafood at a time, dip it into the batter, shake off excess, then lower it into the oil, in batches if necessary. Deep-fry for 2–3 minutes, or until golden and crisp. Drain on crumpled paper towels, then keep warm in a low oven while you cook the rest. Sprinkle with salt and serve with lemon wedges and a tartare sauce. Serves 4.

OYSTER PO' BOYS

To make the batter, sift 60 g (2¼ oz/½ cup) self-raising flour, ¼ teaspoon cayenne pepper, ¼ teaspoon paprika and a pinch of salt into a bowl. Beat 1 small egg and 125 ml (4 fl oz/½ cup) milk together and gradually add to the flour, whisking to give a smooth batter. To use, fill a deep-fryer or large saucepan one-third full of vegetable oil and heat to 180°C (350°F). Pat dry 18 freshly shucked oysters, dip into the batter and deep-fry in batches for 1–2 minutes, or until golden brown. Drain on crumpled paper towels and serve immediately, either as they are or sandwiched between crusty bread. Makes 18.

beer-battered fish with crunchy chips

Thai yellow fish and prawn curry

SERVES 4

Many good-quality ready-made curry pastes are available in the Asian section of most supermarkets. If you'd prefer to use one of these rather than make your own, use 3–4 tablespoons of yellow curry paste and skip the first step.

curry paste	
fresh turmeric	1 tablespoon chopped, or 2 teaspoons ground turmeric
ground coriander	1 teaspoon
ground cumin	1 teaspoon
yellow or red chillies	3 small
lemon grass	1 stem, cut into three pieces
fresh galangal or ginger	a small knob, peeled
coriander (cilantro) root	1 tablespoon chopped
garlic	2 large cloves, peeled
red Asian shallots	2, peeled
dried shrimp paste	1 teaspoon
oil	60 ml (2 fl oz/¼ cup)
coconut milk	800 ml (28 fl oz)
makrut (kaffir lime) leaves	4, optional
lime	finely grated zest and juice of 1
fish sauce	1 tablespoon
palm sugar	1 teaspoon grated, or soft brown sugar
Thai pea eggplants (aubergines)	30 (optional; see note)
Thai or other baby eggplants (aubergines), or regular eggplant	4, quartered, or 150 g (5½ oz), cut into small chunks
bean sprouts	50 g (1¾ oz), trimmed
tiger prawns (shrimp)	12, peeled and deveined, tails intact
lemon sole fillets	600 g (1 lb 5 oz), skinned and cut into bite-sized chunks
Thai basil or other basil leaves	2 tablespoons
coriander (cilantro) leaves	1 tablespoon
steamed rice	to serve

To make curry paste, put the turmeric, ground coriander, cumin, chillies, lemon grass, galangal, coriander root, garlic, shallots, shrimp paste and 60 ml (2 fl oz/¼ cup) water in a small food processor and whizz until a thick paste forms. Alternatively, finely chop all ingredients with a sharp knife or pound in a mortar with a pestle and then mix everything together by hand.

Heat the oil in a large saucepan or wok and add the curry paste. Cook, stirring often, for 5 minutes, or until fragrant. Pour in the coconut milk, then add the lime leaves, lime zest and juice, fish sauce, sugar, Thai pea eggplants (if using) and other eggplant. Stir well, bring the mixture to the boil, then reduce the heat to low, cover with a lid and simmer for 15 minutes, or until the curry has thickened slightly and the eggplant is cooked.

Remove the lid from the pan and add the bean sprouts, prawns and chunks of fish. Cook for 4–5 minutes, or until the prawns have turned a pale pink and the fish is opaque. Stir in the basil and coriander leaves, add a little salt if necessary, and serve with steamed rice.

Fish substitution cod, hapuka, snapper, kingfish, grouper

Note Pea eggplants are very small and round, about the size of a marble. They are sometimes available at Asian grocery stores.

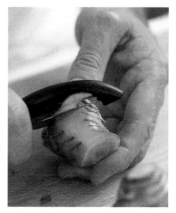

If using fresh turmeric, peel it first, then chop.

Finely grate the zest of the lime, then juice the lime.

Jellyfish salad

This type of recipe falls under the Japanese title aemono, which refers to recipes in which ingredients are coated in a dressing of some kind. Serve this salad as a first course.

dried jellyfish	1oo g (3½ oz), or 1 x 150 g (5½ oz) packet of ready-to-use jellyfish
firm tofu	150 g (5½ oz)
white sesame seeds	3 tablespoons, roasted and crushed
caster (superfine) sugar	2 teaspoons
sake	1 tablespoon
soy sauce	2 tablespoons
rice vinegar	2 tablespoons
cucumber	1½, peeled and cut into thin strips

If using dried jellyfish, put the jellyfish in a bowl and cover with boiling water. Leave to soak for 15 seconds, then drain. Return the jellyfish to the bowl and cover with warm water. Leave to soak for 3 hours, changing the water every hour. Finely slice using a sharp knife or scissors then return to the soaking liquid and set aside until needed. If using packet jellyfish, follow the preparation instructions on the pack.

Put the tofu on a plate and cover with a clean tea towel. Put another plate on top and put a weight, such as a tin, on top of the plate. Leave the tofu to drain for 1 hour.

Tip away any excess liquid that has come out of the tofu and crumble the tofu into a coarse-meshed sieve set over a mixing bowl. Using a wooden spoon, push the tofu through the sieve into the bowl, then add 2 tablespoons of the sesame seeds, the sugar, sake, soy sauce and rice vinegar. Mix until combined, then cover and chill until needed.

Strain jellyfish, discarding the soaking liquid. Rinse and pat dry. Gently mix the jellyfish with tofu dressing and cucumber strips. Serve garnished with remaining sesame seeds.

Shellfish substitution cooked shelled shellfish such as clams, small mussels or small prawns (shrimp)

If using dried jellyfish, first soak it briefly in boiling water.

Drain the jellyfish, then soak it in warm water until soft.

Place a plate and tin on top of the tofu and leave to drain.

Octopus salad

Many recipes for octopus come from Mediterranean countries, where this cephalopod is plentiful. This recipe combines tender simmered octopus with typical Mediterranean flavours to produce a simple salad, perfect for a summer lunch.

baby octopus	650 g (1 lb 7 oz), cleaned
mixed salad leaves	120 g (4¼ oz)
lemon wedges	to serve
dressing	
lemon juice	2 tablespoons
olive oil	100 ml (3½ fl oz)
garlic	1 clove, thinly sliced
mint	1 tablespoon, chopped
flat-leaf (Italian) parsley	1 tablespoon, chopped
dijon mustard	1 teaspoon
cayenne pepper	a pinch

Bring a large saucepan of water to the boil and add the octopus. Simmer for 8–10 minutes, or until the octopus is tender when tested with the point of a knife.

Meanwhile, make the dressing by mixing together lemon juice, olive oil, garlic, mint, parsley, mustard and the cayenne pepper with some salt and freshly ground black pepper.

Drain the octopus well and put in a bowl. Pour the dressing over the top and cool for a few minutes before transferring to the refrigerator. Chill for at least 3 hours before serving on a bed of salad leaves. Drizzle a little of the dressing over the top and serve with lemon wedges.

The octopus has more often filled our imaginations than our stomachs. One species can grow to 10 m (30 ft) from head to tentacle-tip and scientists have proven that octopuses are intelligent, with long- and short-term memories. So, perhaps it is not entirely surprising that many cooks are happier with baby octopus. Apart from size, the main difference between baby octopus and larger ones is the tenderness of the former; it needs neither beating nor blanching before cooking. Baby octopus can be cooked whole and are perfect for barbecuing and adding to salads. Japanese and Mediterranean cooks in particular make excellent use of these tender creatures.

three ways with oysters

To check that oysters are fresh and alive before cooking them or eating them raw, tap any open ones against a surface; discard any that don't close. Scrub oysters well under running water before use, but do not soak them. Unopened, live oysters can be stored for a week in the refrigerator or in a cool place, covered with damp newspaper or damp hessian; once opened, store them in their liquid and eat within 24 hours. Oysters should open once they are cooked; discard any that remain closed.

OYSTERS ROCKEFELLER

Arrange 24 freshly shucked oysters in their half shells on a bed of rock salt or crushed ice on a large platter. Cover and refrigerate until needed. Melt 60 g (2¼ oz) butter in a saucepan. Add 2 finely chopped bacon slices and cook until browned. Add 8 finely chopped spinach leaves, 2 finely chopped spring onions (scallions), 2 tablespoons finely chopped flat-leaf (Italian) parsley, 35 g (1¼ oz/⅓ cup) dry breadcrumbs and a drop of Tabasco sauce. Cook over medium heat until the spinach has wilted. Spoon onto the oysters and grill (broil) under high heat for 2–3 minutes, or until golden. Transfer to a platter lined with rock salt and serve. Serves 4.

OYSTERS WITH WASABI, SOY AND GINGER

Arrange 12 freshly shucked Pacific or other oysters in their half shells on a bed of rock salt or crushed ice on a large platter. Cover and refrigerate until needed. Mix together ⅓ teaspoon wasabi paste, 1 tablespoon dark soy sauce, 1 tablespoon rice wine vinegar and 1 tablespoon finely chopped pink pickled ginger. Drizzle a little sauce over each oyster and serve. Serves 2.

OYSTERS WITH GINGER AND LIME

Arrange 12 freshly shucked oysters in their half shells on a bed of rock salt or crushed ice on a large platter. Cover and refrigerate until needed. Mix together ½ teaspoon finely grated fresh ginger, the zest and juice of 2 limes, 2 teaspoons Thai fish sauce, 1 tablespoon chopped coriander (cilantro) leaves and 2 teaspoons sugar. Drizzle a little sauce over each oyster and serve with lime wedges. Serves 2.

Note Oysters should be opened, or shucked, just before they are to be used. To shuck oysters, you will need an oyster knife. Have ready a tray or platter thickly spread with crushed ice or rock salt, on which the opened oysters can be balanced so that they do not lose any of their flavourful juice. Place the oyster, curved side down, on a flat surface, with the hinged end facing you. Wrap your non-opening hand in a tea towel for protection, then grasp the oyster. With the other hand, insert the blade of the oyster knife into the hinge of the oyster, twisting and pushing the knife to lever off the top shell (this will require quite a bit of force). Discard top shell. Slip the oyster knife between the oyster and the bottom shell and sever the muscle that attaches the flesh to the shell. Carefully place the opened oyster in the prepared tray and remove any shell fragments. Do not wash the oyster, or you will wash away the precious juices. If eating oysters raw, it is usual to swallow them in one gulp, then to drink the delicious briny juices straight from the shell.

oysters rockefeller

Clams in coconut sauce

SERVES 4

There is a bewildering variety of edible clams throughout the world. The small species may be eaten raw; larger ones are best minced (ground) and used in chowders. Small hard-shell or littleneck clams are perfect for this recipe.

French shallots	2, peeled
garlic	1 clove, peeled
lemon grass	6 cm (2½ inch) piece
small red chilli	1
fresh ginger	1 teaspoon grated
candlenuts, unsalted macadamia nuts or peanuts	1 tablespoon, finely chopped
ground cumin	¾ teaspoon
ground coriander	1 teaspoon
palm sugar	1 teaspoon grated, or soft brown sugar
coconut milk	800 ml (28 fl oz)
oil	2 tablespoons
fish sauce	1 tablespoon
lime	juice of 1
fresh or dried coconut	50 g (1¾ oz) shredded
clams	1.5 kg (3 lb 5 oz) small, cleaned (see page 137)

Put shallots, garlic, lemon grass, chilli, ginger, nuts, cumin, coriander, sugar and 60 ml (2 fl oz/¼ cup) of coconut milk in a food processor and blend to a fine paste. Alternatively, chop all ingredients finely and then blend by hand in a bowl. Heat oil in a large saucepan and when hot, add the paste. Cook, stirring, for 5 minutes. Add fish sauce, lime juice, remaining coconut milk and shredded coconut. Bring to the boil, then reduce to a simmer and cook, uncovered, for 10 minutes.

Meanwhile, put the clams in a separate large saucepan with 60 ml (2 fl oz/¼ cup) water. Bring the water to the boil, then cover with a tight-fitting lid and cook over medium heat for 5–7 minutes, or until shells have opened. Drain, discarding the cooking liquid and any clams that have not opened. Add the clams to the coconut sauce. Mix and season with salt. Spoon the clams into 4 deep bowls and spoon the sauce over the top.

Shellfish substitution cockles, pipis, mussels

Palm sugar is a dark, unrefined sugar obtained mostly from the sap of the palmyra palm tree. The sap is collected from the trees, boiled until it turns into a thick, dark syrup, then poured into moulds – traditionally empty coconut shells – where it dries to form dense, heavy cakes. Palm sugar is widely used in sweet and savoury dishes in India and Southeast Asia, particularly Thailand. It goes well with seafood such as salmon and prawns (shrimp). Buy in blocks or in jars from Asian shops and shave off the sugar as you need it. It is also known as jaggery or gur. Soft brown sugar can be substituted if palm sugar is unavailable.

Seafood risotto

SERVES 4

Risotto rice is a special type that can absorb a lot of liquid and still retain its shape. Eat risotto as soon as it is made; it does not reheat well. Italians often form leftover risotto into large balls, known as suppli or arancini, which are crumbed and fried and eaten hot or cold.

fish stock	1.75 litres (61 fl oz/7 cups)
olive oil	2 tablespoons
onions	2, finely chopped
garlic	2 cloves, finely chopped
celery	1 stalk, finely chopped
risotto rice	450 g (1 lb/2 cups)
black mussels	8–10, cleaned
blue-eye cod fillet	150 g (5½ oz), cubed
raw prawns (shrimp)	8, peeled and deveined, tails intact
flat-leaf (Italian) parsley	2 tablespoons chopped
oregano	1 tablespoon chopped
thyme	1 tablespoon chopped
butter	20 g (¾ oz)
zest	of 1 lemon
lemon juice	1–2 teaspoons

Pour the stock into a saucepan and bring to the boil. Reduce the heat until just simmering, then cover.

Heat olive oil in a large saucepan over medium heat. Add the onion, garlic and celery and then cook for 2–3 minutes. Add 2 tablespoons water, cover with a lid and cook for 5 minutes, or until the vegetables soften. Add rice and cook, stirring, over medium heat for 3–4 minutes, until rice grains are well coated.

Gradually add 125 ml (4 fl oz/½ cup) of the hot stock to the rice, stirring over low heat with a wooden spoon, until all the stock has been absorbed. Repeat, adding 125 ml (4 fl oz/½ cup) stock each time until only a small amount of stock is left and the rice is just tender — this should take 20–25 minutes.

Meanwhile, bring 60 ml (2 fl oz/¼ cup) water to the boil in a saucepan. Add mussels, cover with a lid and then cook for about 4–5 minutes, shaking the pan occasionally, until the mussels have opened. Drain and discard any unopened ones. If the mussels are large, remove them from their shells. Set them aside until you're ready to add them to the risotto. Add fish, prawns and the remaining hot stock to rice and stir well. Cook for 5–10 minutes, or until seafood is just cooked and the rice is tender and creamy. Remove from heat, add the mussels, cover and set aside for 5 minutes. Stir parsley, oregano, thyme, butter, lemon zest and lemon juice through risotto, then season to taste with salt and freshly ground black pepper. Leave to rest, covered, for 2 minutes, then serve.

Fish substitution coley, ling, cod

As each batch of liquid is absorbed, add a little more.

Fold the seafood into the risotto and simmer until just cooked.

three ways with mussels

Mussels have been cultivated since ancient Roman times. To prepare them, scrub them well under running water to remove any barnacles and parasites, and pull off the fibrous 'beard'. Discard any mussels that do not close when tapped; these ones are dead and are not safe to eat. As mussels are indiscriminate filter feeders, they can harbour harmful organisms or toxins from polluted waters. If you collect your own, make sure they come from clean waters.

MUSSELS WITH COCONUT MILK BROTH

Halve a lemon grass stalk and squash it a couple of times with the back of a wooden spoon. Grate a 5 cm (2 inch) piece of fresh ginger. Heat 2 tablespoons oil in a large saucepan and gently fry 1 finely chopped onion for 5 minutes. Add lemon grass and ginger, 1 thinly sliced small red chilli, 400 ml (14 fl oz) canned coconut milk and 200 ml (7 fl oz) vegetable stock. Bring to the boil, then reduce the heat, cover and simmer for 20 minutes. Remove lemon grass, return the sauce to the boil and add 1.5 kg (3 lb 5 oz) cleaned mussels. Cover and cook, shaking pan until mussels open. Discard any unopened mussels and serve the mussels with the sauce spooned over. Serves 4.

MUSSELS WITH TOMATO, GARLIC AND LEMON

Heat 1 tablespoon oil in a large saucepan and gently fry 1 finely chopped onion and 2 crushed garlic cloves for 5 minutes. Add 550 g (1 lb 2 oz) seeded and diced firm, vine-ripened tomatoes and 2 tablespoons lemon juice. Cook for 5 minutes, stirring gently occasionally. Add 1.5 kg (3 lb 5 oz) cleaned mussels. Cover and cook, shaking the pan until the mussels open. Discard any unopened mussels. Serve the mussels with the grated zest from 1 large lemon and 2 tablespoons roughly chopped flat-leaf (Italian) parsley sprinkled over. Serves 4.

MUSSELS WITH TANGY BREADCRUMBS AND MAYONNAISE

Grate the zest from 1 lemon and squeeze the juice. Put 100 g (3½ oz/⅓ cup) good-quality mayonnaise into a bowl with 1 tablespoon of the lemon juice and 1 crushed garlic clove. Meanwhile, remove the crusts from 100 g (3½ oz) day-old white crusty bread. Put into a food processor and blend into breadcrumbs. Transfer to a large frying pan and dry-fry until golden. Put into a bowl with the lemon zest and 2 tablespoons finely chopped coriander (cilantro) leaves. Clean and debeard 1 kg (2 lb 4 oz) black mussels. Bring 60 ml (2 fl oz/¼ cup) white wine and 2 tablespoons water to the boil in a large saucepan. Add the mussels and cook, shaking the pan until the mussels open. Discard any unopened mussels. Remove the remaining mussels, shake off any excess liquid and remove the top shell. Loosen the mussel from each shell. Spread each mussel with some of the mayonnaise and sprinkle with breadcrumbs. Serve immediately. Serves 4 as an entrée.

mussels with coconut milk broth

Paella

Paella is perhaps the quintessential Spanish dish. Its basis is rice, saffron and olive oil, but argument can rage over what other ingredients — chicken, seafood, snails, peas, chorizo —should or should not be included. What is without doubt, however, is that it is delicious.

white wine	125 ml (4 fl oz/½ cup)
red onion	1 small, chopped
black mussels	12–16, cleaned
olive oil	125 ml (4 fl oz/½ cup)
chicken breast fillet	1 small, cut into bite-sized pieces
streaky bacon slice	1, finely chopped
garlic	4 cloves, crushed
red capsicum (pepper)	1 small, finely chopped
red onion	½ small, extra, finely chopped
vine-ripened tomato	1, peeled and chopped
chorizo	90 g (3¼ oz), thinly sliced
cayenne pepper	a pinch
paella or short-grain rice	200 g (7 oz/1 cup)
saffron threads	¼ teaspoon
chicken stock	500 ml (17 fl oz/2 cups), heated
peas	80 g (2¾ oz/½ cup) fresh or frozen
raw prawns (shrimp)	12, peeled and deveined
squid	100 g (3½ oz), cleaned and cut into rings
cod fillets	100 g (3½ oz), skinned and cut into bite-sized pieces
flat-leaf (Italian) parsley	2 tablespoons chopped

Heat wine and onion in a large saucepan. Add the mussels, cover and gently shake pan for 4–5 minutes over high heat. After 3 minutes, start removing the opened mussels from the pan and set them aside. At the end of 5 minutes, discard any mussels that have not opened. Drain, reserving the liquid. Strain liquid through a fine sieve lined with muslin (cheesecloth) and reserve.

Heat half the oil in a large frying pan. Pat chicken dry with paper towels, then cook the chicken for 5 minutes, or until golden brown. Remove from the pan and set aside.

Heat remaining oil in the pan, add the bacon, garlic, capsicum and extra red onion and cook for 5 minutes, or until the onion is softened but not browned. Add tomato, chorizo and cayenne pepper. Season with salt and freshly ground black pepper. Stir in the reserved cooking liquid, then add the rice and mix well.

Soak the saffron threads in 125 ml (4 fl oz/½ cup) hot stock, then add this mixture, along with the remaining stock, to the rice and mix well. Bring slowly to the boil. Reduce the heat to low and simmer, uncovered, for 15 minutes, without stirring.

Put the peas, chicken, prawns, squid and fish on top of the rice. Using a wooden spoon, push pieces of the seafood into the rice, cover and cook over low heat for 10 minutes, or until the rice is tender and the seafood is cooked. Add the mussels for the last 5 minutes to heat through. If the rice is not quite cooked, add a little extra stock and cook for a few more minutes. Leave to rest for 5 minutes, covered, then sprinkle with parsley and serve.

Fish substitution ling, mahi mahi, blue-eye, monkfish

Soak the saffron threads in a small amount of hot stock.

Arrange the peas, chicken and seafood over the rice.

Steamed clams with corn and bacon

SERVES 4

In the New England region of the United States, clambakes are cooked on the beach at times of celebration. Clams and other seafood are baked, often accompanied by corn-on-the-cob. This recipe combines clams and corn with a few other flavours.

butter	25 g (1 oz)
onion	1 large, chopped
bacon	100 g (3½ oz), chopped
clams	1.5 kg (3 lb 5 oz), cleaned
corn	1 large cob, kernels removed
dry cider	150 ml (5 fl oz)
thick (double/heavy) cream	150 ml (5 fl oz)

Melt butter in a large saucepan and when hot, add the onion and bacon. Cook over medium heat for about 5 minutes, or until the onion is soft and the bacon cooked.

Tip the clams into a large saucepan with 60 ml (2 fl oz/¼ cup) water and put over medium–high heat. Once the water is hot and the clams begin to steam, cover with a lid and cook for 2–3 minutes, or until they have opened. Drain, reserving the liquid. Strain the liquid through a fine sieve lined with muslin (cheesecloth) and reserve. Discard any unopened clams.

Add the corn kernels to the onion and bacon and cook for 3–4 minutes, or until tender, stirring often. Pour in the cider and 60 ml (2 fl oz/¼ cup) of the reserved cooking liquid. Bring to the boil, then simmer for 2 minutes. Stir in cream and season with salt and freshly ground black pepper. Add clams and toss them through the sauce. Serve in warmed deep bowls.

Shellfish substitution pipis, cockles, mussels

Clams are bivalve molluscs, and are classed as either soft- or hard-shelled. Hard-shelled clams come in different sizes and colours, and most countries stick to their local favourites: the quahog (also called littleneck) is popular in the United States, palourde in France, hamaguri in Japan, and pipis, tuatua and toheroa in Australasia. All are good raw or cooked. Soft-shelled clams, which have brittle shells that gape open, are most common in North America, home of the clambake. This great beachside feast normally features soft-shelled geoduck clams, which have long syphons. Clams must be bought live, then cleaned and shucked just before use.

three ways with squid

The general rule when cookiing squid and octopus is to do so either very briefly or for a very long time — anything in the middle tends to result in tough meat. When buying squid, ready-cleaned squid tubes are the easiest option. If you want to clean and prepare whole squid or octopus yourself, refer to the instructions on page 127. Scoring a criss-cross pattern on the inner surface of squid tubes causes them to curl up into attractive pinecone-like shapes, or flowers, when cooked.

STIR-FRIED SQUID FLOWERS WITH CAPSICUM

Halve lengthways and open out 400 g (14 oz) squid tubes. Wash off any soft jelly-like substance and pat dry. Lay on a chopping board and score the inside of the flesh with a fine crisscross pattern, making sure to not cut all the way through. Cut the squid into pieces that are about 3 x 5 cm (1¼ x 2 inches). Blanch squid in a saucepan of boiling water for 25–30 seconds — each piece will curl up and the crisscross pattern will open out, hence the name 'squid flower'. Remove and refresh in cold water, then drain and dry well. Heat a wok over high heat, add 60 ml (2 fl oz/¼ cup) oil and heat until very hot. Add 2 tablespoons mashed salted and fermented black beans, 1 finely diced small onion, 1 finely diced small green capsicum (pepper), 3–4 small slices peeled fresh ginger, 1 spring onion (scallion), cut into short lengths, and 1 chopped small red chilli. Stir-fry for 1 minute. Add squid and 1 tablespoon Chinese rice wine, blend well and stir for 1 minute. Sprinkle with ½ teaspoon roasted sesame oil. Serves 4 as part of a Chinese banquet or as a starter.

SALT AND PEPPER SQUID

Halve lengthways and open out 1 kg (2 lb 4 oz) squid tubes. Wash off any soft jelly-like substance and pat dry. Lay on a chopping board and score inside of the flesh with a fine crisscross pattern, making sure to not cut all the way through. Cut into pieces about 3 x 5 cm (1¼ x 2 inches). Put in a flat non-metallic dish and pour 250 ml (9 fl oz/1 cup) lemon juice over the top. Cover and then refrigerate for 15 minutes. Drain and pat dry. Combine 250 g (9 oz/2 cups) cornflour (cornstarch), 1½ tablespoons salt, 1 tablespoon ground white pepper and 2 teaspoons caster (superfine) sugar in a bowl. Dip squid into 4 lightly beaten egg whites and then into the flour mixture, shaking off any excess. Fill a deep-fryer or large saucepan one-third full of oil and heat to 180°C (350°F), or until a cube of white bread dropped into the oil turns golden brown in 15 seconds. Cook batches of squid for 1–2 minutes, or until the flesh turns white and curls. Drain on crumpled paper towels. Serve with lemon wedges and garnish with coriander (cilantro) leaves. Serves 6.

MEDITERRANEAN SQUID STEW

Clean 900 g (2 lb) squid (see page 127). Cut the body into rings and roughly chop the tentacles. (Alternatively, buy 450 g/1 lb cleaned squid tubes.) Heat 2 tablespoons olive oil in a frying pan over medium heat. Add 1 chopped onion and cook for 5 minutes. Add 1 seeded and finely chopped red capsicum (pepper) and 2 crushed garlic cloves and cook for 2–3 minutes. Add 125 ml (4 fl oz/½ cup) white wine, 600 g (1 lb 5 oz) canned chopped tomatoes and 1 tablespoon tomato purée (concentrated paste). Bring to the boil. Stir in the squid, reduce the heat and simmer, covered, for 50 minutes. Add 50 g (1¾ oz) pitted and halved black olives and a handful of flat-leaf (Italian) parsley leaves. Cook, covered, for 10 more minutes, or until the squid is tender. Serve with rice. Serves 4.

stir-fried squid flowers with capsicum

Spaghetti alle vongole

SERVES 4

Vongole is simply the Italian word for clam. Clams vary in size and shape from region to region; ask your fishmonger for the best local variety. Even if they are sold as cleaned, it's worth giving them an extra clean yourself: see page 137 for instructions on how to do this.

olive oil	2 tablespoons
garlic	3 cloves, crushed
chilli flakes	2 pinches
dry white wine	125 ml (4 fl oz/½ cup)
canned chopped tomatoes	400 g (14 oz)
flat-leaf (Italian) parsley	3 tablespoons finely chopped
clams	1 kg (2 lb 4 oz), cleaned
dried spaghetti or linguine	400 g (14 oz)
lemon zest	½ teaspoon grated
lemon halves	to serve

Heat the oil in a large, deep frying pan. Add the garlic and chilli and cook over low heat for 30 seconds. Add the white wine, tomatoes and 1 teaspoon of the parsley. Increase the heat and boil, stirring occasionally, for 8–10 minutes, or until the liquid is reduced by half.

Add the clams to the pan and cover with a lid. Increase the heat and cook for 3–5 minutes, or until the clams have opened, shaking the pan often. Remove the clams from the pan, discarding any that have not opened. Stir in the remaining parsley and season. Boil the sauce for 3–4 minutes until thick. Set half the clams aside and extract the meat from the rest.

Cook the pasta in a large saucepan of boiling salted water until al dente. Drain and stir through the sauce. Add the lemon zest, reserved clams and clam meat and toss well. Serve with the lemon halves.

Shellfish substitution pipis, small mussels

Pasta is one of the world's great foods. Cheap, durable in its dried form and endlessly versatile, it has been adopted by cooks the world over. The types and shapes of pasta are many: tiny stars, long strands or ribbons, large shells, and dozens more. Long, thin pastas, which include spaghetti and linguine, are excellent for serving with simple sauces that will stick to their lengths without falling off, or with seafood such as clams, as the clams can be easily picked out and the flesh removed from the shells. Spaghetti alle vongole is a classic seafood and pasta combination; although, in fact, most shellfish is delicious with pasta.

Moules marinières

SERVES 6

'A la mariniere' is a French term denoting a dish in which seafood, especially mussels, is cooked in white wine, usually with onions or shallots. The following is a quick and classic way to prepare mussels. Serve them with plenty of bread to sop up the delicious juices.

butter	50 g (1¾ oz)
onion	1 large, chopped
celery	½ stalk, chopped
garlic	2 cloves, crushed
white wine	400 ml (14 fl oz)
bay leaf	1
thyme	2 sprigs
mussels	2 kg (4 lb 8 oz), cleaned (see page 173)
thick (double/heavy) cream	220 ml (7½ fl oz)
flat-leaf (Italian) parsley	2 tablespoons, chopped
crusty bread	to serve

Melt butter in a large saucepan over medium heat. Add the onion, celery and garlic and cook, stirring occasionally, for anout 5 minutes, or until onion is softened but not browned.

Add the wine, bay leaf and thyme to the saucepan and bring to the boil. Add the mussels, cover the pan tightly and simmer over low heat for 2–3 minutes, shaking pan occasionally. Using tongs or a slotted spoon, lift out the mussels as they open and put them into a warm dish. Discard any mussels that haven't opened after 3 minutes.

Strain cooking liquid through a muslin-lined fine sieve into a clean saucepan to remove any grit or sand. Bring the liquid to the boil and boil for 2 minutes. Add the cream and reheat without boiling. Season well. Serve the mussels in individual bowls with the liquid poured over. Sprinkle with the parsley and serve with plenty of bread.

As the mussels open, remove them and place in a warmed dish.

Strain the liquid through a sieve lined with muslin into a clean pan.

three ways with scallops

Scallops are found in all seas. The many species can all be cooked in the same ways, or eaten raw. All have fan-shaped shells, white meat and edible orange-red roe. If bought opened but still on the half-shell, they will need to be rinsed, as they can be sandy. If bought whole, they will need to be scrubbed. Discard any that are open but do not close quickly when sharply tapped. Once cooked, the shells should open up; discard any that remain closed.

SCALLOP CEVICHE

Clean 16 scallops in their closed shells by scrubbing under running water. One by one, hold the scallop in a tea towel and, with a sharp knife or an oyster knife, carefully prise open the shell. Lift off the top shell and loosen the scallop from the shell. Pull off and discard the scallop's outer grey fringe and outer membrane. Retain the shells. In a non-metallic bowl, mix together 1 teaspoon finely grated lime zest, 60 ml (2 fl oz/¼ cup) lime juice, 2 chopped garlic cloves, 2 seeded and chopped red chillies, 1 tablespoon chopped coriander (cilantro) leaves and 1 tablespoon olive oil. Season with salt and freshly ground black pepper. Put scallops in the dressing and stir to coat. Cover with plastic wrap and refrigerate for 2 hours; the acid in the lime juice will 'cold-cook' the scallop flesh. To serve, slide each scallop back onto a half shell and spoon a little of the lime dressing over it. Top each scallop with a whole coriander leaf. Serve cold. For an attractive presentation, the scallops in their half shells can be placed on a bed of rock salt or crushed ice on a large platter. Serves 4.

SCALLOPS IN BLACK BEAN SAUCE

Clean 24 scallops in their closed shells by scrubbing under running water. Heat 1 tablespoon oil in a wok and, when hot, add the scallops. Cook for 2 minutes, or until just firm. (Do not overcook, or they will be tough and rubbery.) Transfer to a plate. Mix together 1 tablespoon soy sauce, 2 tablespoons Chinese rice wine, 1 teaspoon sugar and 1 tablespoon water and set aside. Add another 1 tablespoon oil to the wok and heat until it is beginning to smoke. Add 1 finely chopped garlic clove, 1 finely chopped spring onion (scallion) and ½ teaspoon finely grated fresh ginger. Cook for 30 seconds. Add 1 tablespoon rinsed and drained salted fermented black beans and the reserved soy sauce mixture and bring to the boil. Return the scallops to the sauce with 1 teaspoon roasted sesame oil and allow to simmer for about 30 seconds. Serve immediately with rice and steamed Asian greens. Serves 4.

Shellfish substitution prawns (shrimp), crayfish or lobster, baby squid

BARBECUED ASIAN-STYLE SCALLOPS

Put 300 g (10½ oz) scallop meat in a shallow non-metallic bowl. In a separate bowl, combine 80 ml (2½ fl oz/⅓ cup) sweet chilli sauce, 1 teaspoon fish sauce, 2 teaspoons lime juice and 1 teaspoon peanut oil. Pour the mixture over the scallop meat and mix gently to coat. Allow to marinate for 1 hour. Drain the seafood well and reserve the marinade. Preheat a barbecue flatplate to high, add 1 tablespoon peanut oil and heat. Cook the scallops for 3–5 minutes, or until tender. Drizzle with a little of the leftover marinade during cooking. Serve on a bed of steamed rice with wedges of lime. Serves 2.

scallop ceviche

Laksa lemak

A robustly flavoured soup, laksa is a meal in itself. It features rice noodles, seafood or chicken and various garnishes in a spicy stock. Laksa lemak, the Singaporean version, is rich with coconut milk and is the most popular type.

rice noodles	115 g (4 oz)
unsalted macadamias	50 g (1¾ oz)
oil	1 tablespoon
canned coconut milk	800 ml (28 fl oz)
lime juice	80 ml (2½ fl oz/⅓ cup)
bean sprouts	115 g (4 oz), trimmed
large raw prawns (shrimp)	20, peeled and deveined
large scallops	16, cleaned
Vietnamese mint	a handful, shredded, a few leaves left whole to garnish
Lebanese (short) cucumber	½, peeled and thinly sliced

paste
red chillies	3, seeded and chopped
lemon grass	2 stems
fresh ginger	a small knob, grated
red Asian shallots	4, peeled
shrimp paste	3 teaspoons
ground turmeric	3 teaspoons

Soak the rice noodles in boiling water for 10 minutes. Drain.

To make paste, put all the paste ingredients, plus 1 tablespoon water, into a food processor and blend until smooth. If you don't have a food processor, finely chop by hand and mix well.

Put the nuts in a saucepan and dry-roast over medium heat, shaking the pan, until golden. Transfer to a plate.

Heat the oil in the same saucepan, add the prepared paste and cook over medium heat for 2 minutes. Stir in the coconut milk, then gently simmer for 10 minutes, or until it thickens slightly. Roughly chop the nuts.

When the coconut milk mixture is ready, add the lime juice and three-quarters of the bean sprouts to the pan. Season with salt, bring back to a simmer, then add the prawns and scallops and cook for about 5 minutes, or until the prawns have turned pink. Add the shredded mint and the noodles. Mix the whole mint leaves with the chopped nuts and cucumber.

Ladle into 4 deep bowls, then sprinkle with the remaining bean sprouts and the mint and cucumber mixture.

Fish substitution cubes of any firm-fleshed white fish

Soak the rice noodles in boiling water to soften them.

Stir the coconut milk into the fried spice paste.

Spaghetti with seafood

Seafood pasta in many restaurants around the world is erroneously termed marinara. Marinara is traditionally the sauce made by Italian fishing families, to which the day's catch would be added. So the name, in fact, refers to the sauce, not the seafood.

tomato sauce

olive oil	2 tablespoons
onion	1, finely chopped
carrot	1, finely chopped
garlic	2 cloves, crushed
canned chopped tomatoes	400 g (14 oz)
white wine	125 ml (4 fl oz/½ cup)
sugar	1 teaspoon
white wine	60 ml (2 fl oz/¼ cup)
fish stock	60 ml (2 fl oz/¼ cup)
garlic	1 clove, crushed
black mussels	12, cleaned (optional)
clams	400 g, cleaned, or 200 g (7 oz) canned, drained
spaghetti	375 g (13 oz)
butter	30 g (1 oz)
squid tubes	125 g (4½ oz), cleaned and cut into rings
cod fillet	125 g (4½ oz), skinned and cut into bite-sized pieces
raw prawns (shrimp)	200 g (7 oz), peeled and deveined, tails left on
flat-leaf (Italian) parsley	a large handful, chopped

To make the tomato sauce, heat the oil in a saucepan, add the onion and carrot and cook over medium heat for 10 minutes, or until lightly browned. Add the garlic, tomato, white wine and sugar, bring to the boil, then reduce the heat and gently simmer for 30 minutes, stirring occasionally.

Heat wine, stock and garlic in a large saucepan. Add mussels and clams (if using clams in the shell). Cover and shake the pan over high heat for 5 minutes. After 3 minutes, start removing any opened mussels and clams and set them aside. After a total of 5 minutes, discard any unopened mussels and clams. Strain the cooking liquid through a fine sieve lined with muslin (cheesecloth) and reserve.

Cook the spaghetti in a large saucepan of boiling salted water until al dente. Drain and keep warm.

Meanwhile, melt butter in a frying pan and stir-fry the squid, cod and prawns in batches for 2 minutes, or until just cooked. Remove from the heat and add to the tomato sauce, along with the reserved cooking liquid, mussels, parsley and clams (in the shell or canned). Gently heat through, then toss the sauce with the pasta and serve.

Fish substitution haddock, plaice or any firm white fish

Add the garlic, tomato, wine and sugar to the carrot and onion.

Fry the squid, cod and prawns in batches in the melted butter.

Add the seafood and remaining ingredients to the tomato sauce.

the perfect mussel

Mussels are bivalve molluscs that are stored and cooked live. Once they die they deteriorate rapidly, so care should be taken in their storing and cooking. The best practice is to put them in a bowl and then cover them with a damp tea towel — do not store them in water, as they will die. Keep them in the bottom of the refrigerator, preferably in the salad compartment, at around 2°C (35°F). They should last a couple of days like this, but it is preferable to eat them on the day of purchase.

Mussels must be cleaned well before cooking, as they are filter feeders and hence can be quite gritty. Put the mussels in a sink full of cold water and clean them one by one. Using a small sharp knife, remove any barnacles and pull away the hairy 'beard'. This is what the mussel uses to hang on to the rock or rope when growing. Discard any mussels with broken shells. Tap open mussels on the work surface to close them. If they do not close they are probably dead, so discard them. Also discard any particularly heavy ones, as they might be full of sand. Once cleaned, rinse the mussels one or two more times and cook as soon as possible after cleaning. Once again, do not store them in water if not cooking immediately.

The best way to cook mussels is to steam them open in a large saucepan. Bring about 1 cm (½ inch) water, white wine or other cooking liquid to the boil, along with any other flavouring, such as garlic, onion or herbs, stirred through. Add mussels, cover tightly with the lid and cook for a couple of minutes, shaking pan regularly. Remove any mussels that have opened, then cook for another minute to open the rest. Discard any mussels that do not open, as they are probably dead. Eat mussels immediately, with or without the cooking liquid.

Marmite dieppoise

The combination of cider and cream in this seafood stew reveals its French origins — from the region of Normandy. Traditionally turbot and sole are used, but salmon adds a splash of colour. The dish takes its name from the iron or earthenware pot in which it is traditionally cooked.

salmon fillet	300 g (10½ oz), skinned
sole fillet	400 g (14 oz), skinned
cider or dry white wine	455 ml (16 fl oz)
mussels	16, cleaned
butter	50 g (1¾ oz)
garlic	1 clove, crushed
French shallots	2, finely chopped
celery	2 stalks, finely chopped
leek	1 large, white part only, thinly sliced
chestnut mushrooms	250 g (9 oz) small, sliced
large raw prawns (shrimp)	12, peeled and deveined
bay leaf	1
thick (double/heavy) cream	300 ml (10½ fl oz)
flat-leaf (Italian) parsley	3 tablespoons, finely chopped

Cut the salmon fillet into bite-sized chunks and cut the sole into thick strips widthways. Set aside until needed.

Pour the cider or white wine into a large saucepan and bring to a simmer. Add the mussels, cover, and cook for 3–5 minutes, shaking the pan occasionally. Put a fine sieve over a large bowl and tip the mussels into the sieve. Transfer mussels to a plate, throwing away any that haven't opened during cooking. Line the sieve with muslin and strain the cooking liquid again to get rid of any grit or sand.

Add the butter to the cleaned saucepan and melt over moderate heat. Add the garlic, shallot, celery and leek and cook, stirring occasionally, for 7–10 minutes, or until the vegetables are just soft. Add the mushrooms and cook for a further 4–5 minutes, or until softened. While the vegetables are cooking, remove the mussels from their shells. You may want to save 6 mussels to use as a garnish.

Add strained cooking liquid and bay leaf to the vegetables in the saucepan and bring to a simmer. Add the salmon, sole and prawns and cook for 3–4 minutes, or until the fish is opaque and the prawns have turned pink. Stir in the cream and cooked mussels and simmer gently for 2 minutes. Season to taste and stir in the parsley. Divide among 6 bowls and garnish each with a reserved mussel, if you wish.

Remove the fibrous beards from the mussels.

Steam the mussels in the cider or wine until they open.

Remove the mussel meat from the shells.

Gumbo

SERVES 6

A speciality of the Cajun cuisine of Louisiana, in the Southern United States, gumbo is a cross between a soup and a stew. Its basis is a dark roux, a slowly cooked and browned amalgam of flour and oil or lard, which is what gives it its rich flavour and colour.

roux	
oil	80 ml (2½ fl oz/⅓ cup)
plain (all-purpose) flour	75 g (2½ oz/scant ⅔ cup)
onion	1, finely chopped
chorizo sausage	450 g (1 lb), cut into bite-sized pieces
spring onions (scallions)	6, sliced
green capsicum (pepper)	1, roughly chopped
flat-leaf (Italian) parsley	3 tablespoons, chopped
chilli powder	¼ teaspoon
cooked crabs	4, cleaned (see page 124) and cut into small pieces
prawns (shrimp)	500 g (1 lb 2 oz), peeled and deveined
oysters	24, freshly shucked
long-grain rice	1½ tablespoons
fill powder	½ teaspoon (see note)

To make the roux, pour oil into a large heavy-based saucepan over low heat. Gradually add flour, stirring after each addition, to make a thin roux. Continue to cook and stir over a low heat for 35 minutes, or until it turns dark brown. Add the onion and cook for 4 minutes, or until tender. Gradually pour in 1.5 litres (52 fl oz/6 cups) boiling water, continually stirring to dissolve the roux, and bring to a simmer.

Add the sausage, spring onion, capsicum, parsley and chilli powder to the roux. Cook for 30 minutes, then add the crab pieces, the prawns and oysters and their juices and cook for another 5 minutes, or until the prawns are pink.

Cook the rice in salted boiling water for about 10 minutes, or until just cooked through. Put a couple of tablespoons of rice in the bottom of each serving bowl.

Just before you are ready to serve the gumbo, season it with salt and freshly ground black pepper, then stir in the filé powder. Do not reheat after the filé is added, or the gumbo will become stringy. Ladle gumbo over rice in the bowls and serve at once.

Note Filé powder is a flavouring and thickening agent often used in Creole and Cajun cooking. It is made by drying and then grinding sassafras leaves. Look for it in speciality food stores or in specialist herb stores.

Stir the flour into the oil and cook over low heat for 35 minutes.

Gradually add the boiling water to the roux.

Continually stir the mixture to dissolve the roux.

Sea urchin roes with spaghetti

SERVES 4

Many sea urchin species are found around the world. Most often, it is the orange roes that are eaten. They are at their best when ripe, just before breeding. Sea urchin roes are traditionally served raw, accompanied by merely a squeeze of fresh lemon juice.

olive oil	60 ml (2 fl oz/¼ cup)
French shallots	2, finely chopped
spaghetti	500 g (1 lb 2 oz)
lemon zest	1 tablespoon, finely grated
flat-leaf (Italian) parsley	2 tablespoons, finely chopped
sea urchin	the roes of 6

Heat the olive oil in a frying pan and when hot, add the shallot. Cook over medium heat for 5 minutes, stirring occasionally, until softened and lightly browned.

Cook the spaghetti in a saucepan of boiling salted water until al dente. Drain and return to the pan.

To make gremolata, combine lemon zest and parsley. Add, along with the oil and shallots, to the pasta. Season with salt and ground black pepper and toss together. Serve in large, shallow bowls with sea urchin roes arranged over the top.

The unusual-looking sea urchin is best described by explaining that its name 'urchin' comes from the old English word for hedgehog. Hidden inside this protective armoury are five orange roe (corals), considered a delicacy in France and Japan. To open a sea urchin, cut a round piece out of the top the shell (the end opposite the mouth) with kitchen scissors. Lift off the piece of shell and drain any juices. Carefully scoop out the roes. They can be eaten as they are, with lemon juice; incorporated into omelettes; or added to creamy sauces to serve with fish. The Japanese make an expensive sea urchin paste.

Zanzibar pilau with squid and prawns

SERVES 4

The legacy left by Arab traders is clear in the availability and popularity of so many wonderful spices in Zanzibar, a beautiful archipelago in the Indian ocean, off the coast of Tanzania. This aromatic rice dish is redolent of those rich, warm flavours.

cinnamon	1 stick
cloves	6
cardamom	6 pods
coriander seeds	½ teaspoon
black peppercorns	½ teaspoon
oil	3 tablespoons
onions	2 large, finely chopped
garlic	3 cloves, finely chopped
ginger	2 teaspoons finely chopped
basmati rice	250 g (9 oz)
vegetable stock	570 ml (20 fl oz)
tomatoes	3, chopped
raisins	150 g (5½ oz)
baby squid	450 g (1 lb), cleaned (see page 127), tentacles left intact
raw prawns (shrimp)	450 g (1 lb), peeled and deveined, tails left on

Put the cinnamon, cloves, cardamom pods, coriander seeds and black peppercorns in a large cup or mug and cover with about 300 ml (10½ fl oz) hot water. Leave to infuse for at least 30 minutes.

Heat 2 tablespoons of the oil in a large sauté or frying pan, add the onion and cook over medium heat for 10 minutes, stirring occasionally, until softened. Add garlic and ginger and cook, stirring, for a further 2 minutes. Add rice and stir to coat with the oil. Add the spices, their liquid and the stock, bring to the boil then reduce the heat, cover the pan and cook for 5 minutes, stirring occasionally. Add the tomatoes and the raisins, re-cover and cook, stirring occasionally, for a further 8–10 minutes, or until the rice is tender. If the rice appears to be drying out, add a little more boiling water. Season to taste then remove the pan from the heat.

Cut the squid tentacles off where they join the body and reserve them. Cut the squid tubes open. Using a sharp knife, score a fine crisscross pattern on the inside of each tube, being careful not to cut all the way through the tubes. Halve or quarter the tubes.

Season the prawns and squid thoroughly with salt and pepper. Heat the remaining tablespoon of oil in a frying pan and cook the prawns for 2–3 minutes. Pile the pilau onto a serving dish and place the prawns on top. Quickly cook the squid in the frying pan for 30–60 seconds on each side, adding a little more oil if necessary. Place on top of the pilau and serve.

Pour boiling water over the spices and allow them to infuse.

Add the spices, their liquid and the stock to the rice.

Asian prawn and noodle salad

SERVES 4

This dish is the work of minutes, yet substantial and delicious. Simplify it even further by buying cooked, peeled prawns (shrimp). Kecap manis is an Indonesian marinade, flavouring and condiment. It resembles soy sauce, but is thicker and sweeter, and usually contains star anise and garlic.

dressing

ginger	2 tablespoons, grated
soy sauce	2 tablespoons
sesame oil	2 tablespoons
red wine vinegar	80 ml (2½ fl oz/⅓ cup)
sweet chilli sauce	1 tablespoon
garlic	2 cloves, crushed
kecap manis	80 ml (2½ fl oz/⅓ cup)
dried instant egg noodles	250 g (9 oz)
cooked large prawns (shrimp)	500 g (1 lb 2 oz), peeled and deveined, tails intact
spring onions (scallions)	5, sliced on the diagonal
coriander (cilantro)	2 tablespoons, chopped
red capsicum (pepper)	1, diced
snow peas (mangetout)	100 g (3½ oz), cut into halves
lime wedges	to serve

For the dressing, whisk together the ginger, soy sauce, sesame oil, vinegar, chilli sauce, garlic and kecap manis in a large bowl.

Cook the egg noodles in a large saucepan of boiling water for 2 minutes, or until tender, then drain thoroughly. Cool in a large serving bowl.

Add the dressing, prawns, spring onions, coriander, capsicum, and snow peas to the noodles and toss gently. Serve with the lime wedges.

Though fresh ginger does not look like much, this knobbly, beige-coloured tropical rhizome is indispensable in much seafood cooking due to its pungent and cleansing flavour. Fresh ginger is a classic ingredient in Chinese steamed fish dishes, Japanese broths and Indian spice pastes and rubs for fish, and it is a more than equal partner for the rich ingredients used in fish stews and soups, such as coconut milk, chilli, nuts and coriander (cilantro). Store fresh ginger in the refrigerator tightly wrapped in plastic wrap; peel and chop or grate before use. Ginger is also available in powdered, dried, pickled, crystallized or preserved forms.

Seafood lasagne

SERVES 6

Lasagne, a classic comfort food, works equally well with seafood as with meat, with the bonus that a seafood sauce takes much less time to cook than its meat counterpart.

olive oil	1 tablespoon
butter	30 g (1 oz)
onion	1, finely chopped
garlic	2 cloves, crushed
small raw prawns (shrimp)	400 g (14 oz), peeled and deveined
firm white fish fillets	500 g (1 lb 2 oz), skinned and cut into 2 cm (¾ inch) pieces
scallops	250 g (9 oz), with roe, cleaned
canned diced tomatoes	800 g (1 lb 12 oz)
tomato paste (concentrated purée)	2 tablespoons
soft brown sugar	1 teaspoon
cheddar cheese	60 g (2¼ oz/½ cup), grated
parmesan cheese	25 g (1 oz/¼ cup), grated
fresh lasagne sheets	250 g (9 oz)
salad	to serve

cheese sauce

butter	120 g (4½ oz)
plain (all-purpose) flour	85 g (3 oz/⅔ cup)
milk	1.5 litres (52 fl oz/6 cups)
cheddar cheese	250 g (9 oz/2 cups), grated
parmesan cheese	100 g (3½ oz/1 cup), grated

Preheat the oven to 180°C (350°F/Gas 4). Grease a 27 x 21 cm (10¾ x 8¼ inch), 2.5 litre (87 fl oz/10 cup) ovenproof dish.

Heat the oil and butter in a large saucepan. Add the onion and cook for 2–3 minutes, or until softened but not browned. Add garlic and cook for 30 seconds, or until fragrant. Add the prawns and fish pieces and cook for 2 minutes before adding the scallops. Cook for a further minute. Stir in the tomatoes, tomato paste and sugar and simmer for 5 minutes.

Combine the grated cheddar and parmesan cheeses in a bowl and set aside until needed for topping the lasagne.

To make the cheese sauce, melt the butter over low heat in a saucepan, then stir in the flour and cook for 1 minute, or until the mixture is pale and foaming. Remove the pan from the heat and gradually stir in the milk. Return the pan to the heat and stir until the sauce boils and thickens. Reduce the heat, simmer for 2 minutes, then stir in the cheddar and parmesan cheeses. Season to taste with salt and freshly ground black pepper.

Line the ovenproof dish with a layer of lasagne sheets. Spoon half of the seafood sauce over the lasagne sheets, spreading it over the pasta. Arrange another layer of lasagne sheets over the top. Top with half of the cheese sauce. Repeat with more lasagne sheets, remaining seafood sauce, a final layer of pasta sheets and the remaining cheese sauce, then sprinkle the top with the combined cheddar and parmesan cheeses. Bake for 30 minutes, or until the top is golden. Leave for 10 minutes to firm up before slicing. Serve with a salad.

Fish substitution hake, snapper, flake, gemfish, ling

Stir the flour into the melted butter and cook for 1 minute.

Add the milk and cook, stirring, until the sauce thickens.

Matelote Normande

A matelote is traditionally the name given to a fish stew, especially one containing eel. Its name is derived from the French word for sailor, matelot. This version uses cider, which is made and commonly used for cooking in the Normandy region of France.

mixed firm white fish fillets, such as turbot or cod steaks	700 g (1 lb 9 oz), skinned
olive oil	80 ml (2½ fl oz/⅓ cup)
white bread	50 g (1¾ oz), crusts removed and cut into cubes
butter	70 g (2½ oz), softened
French shallots or button onions	8, cut in halves if large
button mushrooms	250 g (9 oz), cut in halves or quarters if large
garlic	1 large clove, finely chopped
large scallops	8, white meat and roes separated
dry cider	400 ml (14 fl oz)
bouquet garni	1
flour	1 tablespoon
thick (double/heavy) cream	150 ml (5 fl oz)
flat-leaf (Italian) parsley	2 tablespoons, finely chopped

Cut the fish into bite-sized chunks and set aside. Preheat the oven to 140°C (275°F/Gas 1). To make croutons, heat 60 ml (2 fl oz/¼ cup) oil in a large frying pan. When hot, add the bread in batches and fry for 2 minutes, or until golden brown, stirring as they cook so the croutons brown evenly. Drain on paper towels.

Melt 25g (1 oz) of the butter and the remaining oil in the frying pan and when hot, add the shallots. Cook for 5 minutes over medium heat, then add mushrooms and cook for 10 minutes, stirring occasionally. When cooked, put in a dish, cover with foil and keep warm.

Meanwhile, melt another 25 g (1 oz) of the butter in a large sauté pan and when hot, add the garlic. Cook for 30 seconds, then reduce the heat and add the fish (not the scallops) and cook for 2–3 minutes on each side, turning occasionally.

Cut the white scallop meat in half widthways. Add the cider and bouquet garni to the fish, bring to a simmer and add white scallop meat. Cook gently for 2 minutes. Add scallop roes and cook for a further minute. Remove all the seafood from the liquid and keep warm.

Blend the remaining butter with the flour in a cup to make a paste. Bring cider mixture to the boil again and whisk in the butter and flour paste to the liquid, bit by bit, and allow the sauce to thicken. Simmer for 1 minute, then stir cream into the sauce. Heat through and season to taste.

Return the seafood to the pan. Remove the bouquet garni. Serve, along with the shallots, button mushrooms, croutons and parsley.

Fish substitution rock salmon (huss), halibut or any other firm white fish

Fry the bread in the oil until golden brown on all sides.

Whisk the butter and flour paste into the cider mixture.

Moqueça de peixe

SERVES 4

This is a simple, delicious seafood stew from the province of Bahia, in the northeast of Brazil. The cooking of the region has been heavily influenced by the Portuguese and by the huge number of slaves that they brought with them from Guinea and Sudan in the early 19th century.

fish steaks such as mahi mahi, bream or halibut	4 x 200 g (7 oz)
raw large prawns (shrimp)	8, peeled and deveined
lime juice	60 ml (2 fl oz/¼ cup)
olive oil	2 tablespoons
onion	1 large, finely chopped
garlic	4 large cloves, crushed
red capsicum (pepper)	1 large, seeded and chopped
habañero chilli	1, seeded and finely chopped
vine-ripened tomatoes	500 g (1 lb 2 oz)
coconut milk	300 ml (10½ fl oz)
coriander (cilantro) leaves	3 tablespoons, chopped

Put fish and prawns in a shallow non-metallic dish. Drizzle the lime juice over the seafood. Season with salt and freshly ground black pepper and turn the fish in the juice. Cover and leave for 30 minutes in the refrigerator.

Meanwhile, heat the oil in a large saucepan and add the onion. Cook for 8–10 minutes, until softened. Add the garlic, capsicum and chilli and then cook for a further 3 minutes, stirring occasionally.

Score a cross in the base of each tomato. Put into boiling water for 20 seconds, then plunge into cold water. Drain and peel the skin away from the cross. Chop the tomatoes, discarding the cores and seeds.

Add tomato to the pan and cook for 10 minutes. Allow to cool slightly, then tip the sauce into a food processor or blender and whizz until smooth. Alternatively, push the mixture through a coarse sieve or mouli by hand. Return sauce to the pan. Add coconut milk and bring to a gentle simmer. Lift the fish and the prawns out of the dish and add to the pan, leaving behind any remaining marinade. Cook for 4 minutes or until opaque. Season to taste with salt and freshly ground black pepper and sprinkle the coriander over the top.

Fish substitution sole, cod, bass

Score a cross in the base of each tomato..

Plunge the tomato into cold water to stop further cooking..

Peel the skin away from the cross and discard..

Index

Published in 2010 by Murdoch Books Pty Limited.

Murdoch Books Australia
Pier 8/9, 23 Hickson Road, Millers Point NSW 2000
Phone: +61 (0)2 8220 2000 Fax: +61 (0)2 8220 2558
www.murdochbooks.com.au

Murdoch Books UK Limited
Erico House, 6th Floor North, 93–99 Upper Richmond Road
Putney, London SW15 2TG
Phone: + 44 (0) 20 8785 5995 Fax: + 44 (0) 20 8785 5985
www.murdochbooks.co.uk

Chief Executive: Juliet Rogers

Publisher: Lynn Lewis
Senior Designer: Heather Menzies
Designer: Jacqueline Richards
Editor: Justine Harding
Editorial Coordinator: Liz Malcolm
Text: Margaret Malone, Katy Holder
Recipes: Murdoch Books Test Kitchen
Photographer: Prue Ruscoe, Ashley Mackevicius
Food preparation: Julie Ray, Ross Dobson
Production: Kita George

National Library of Australia Cataloguing-in-Publication Data
Title: Seafood.
ISBN: 978-1-74196-959-7 (pbk.)
Series: Food for Friends.
Notes: Includes index.
Subjects: Cookery (Seafood).
Dewey Number: 641.692

Printed by 1010 Printing International Limited. PRINTED IN CHINA.

IMPORTANT: Those who might be at risk from the effects of salmonella poisoning (the elderly, pregnant women, young children and those suffering from immune deficiency diseases) should consult their doctor with any concerns about eating raw eggs.

CONVERSION GUIDE: You may find cooking times vary depending on the oven you are using. For fan-forced ovens, as a general rule, set the oven temperature to 20°C (70°F) lower than indicated in the recipe. We have used 20 ml (4 teaspoon) tablespoon measures. If you are using a 15 ml (3 teaspoon) tablespoon, for most recipes the difference will not be noticeable. However, for recipes using baking powder, gelatine, bicarbonate of soda, small amounts of flour and cornflour (cornstarch), add an extra teaspoon for each tablespoon specified.